HIS FOOTSTOOL

The Door to Your Destiny

Angela Brown

Dream Gate Publishing

Marietta, Georgia

Dream Gate Publishing
1475 Kolb Lane
Marietta, Georgia 30064
awbrown1@bellsouth.net

Unless otherwise indicated, all scripture quotations are taken from the New King James Version®. Copyright © 1982 by Thomas Nelson, Inc. Used by permission. All rights reserved.
Scripture quotations from The Message. Copyright © by Eugene H. Peterson 2002. Used by permission of NavPress Publishing Group.
Scripture quotations taken from the Amplified® Bible, Copyright © 1954, 1958, 1962, 1964, 1965, 1987 by The Lockman Foundation. Used by permission.
Scripture quotations taken from The Psalms: Poetry on Fire, The Passion Translation®, copyright © 2014. Used by permission of BroadStreet Publishing Group, LLC, Racine, Wisconsin, USA. All rights reserved.

Cover Design: Sarah Delaney
Book Editing: RJF Writing Services
Book Layout © 2014 BookDesignTemplates.com

His Footstool/Angela Brown. -- 1st ed.
ISBN 978-0-9970325-0-5

Early Praise for *His Footstool*

His Footstool will lead you into your own personal place of worship and inspiration. Take your time as you read it to consider and meditate on all the "Questions for Reflection" at the end of each chapter, giving your attention to God's Word and inclining your ear to hear His voice. Here in this secret place with Him, you will experience spiritual growth and emotional healing and preparation for each day. The Holy Spirit will show you things to come as He leads you into a more intimate relationship with Jesus, and you'll discover that to know Jesus is to know the Father. The Creator of the universe has a special, secret place carved out just for you, and there He will walk with you and talk with you. Thank you, Angela, for sharing your personal journey of intimacy with the One who was, the One who is, and the One who is to come.

Germaine Griffin Copeland
Best-selling Author of *Prayers That Avail Much* and other
books on prayer
President & Founder of Word Ministries, Inc.,
Monroe, Georgia

I have known Angela for over 30 years and have appreciated her gift to reveal and convey the Majesty of God in ways that will lift you higher. Her heart chases after the attributes of God and this book is no exception! Join in the chase.

Pat Gastineau
Founder and Teacher at Word of Love Ministries in
Woodstock, Georgia

'I have found David, son of Jesse, a man after my own heart; he will do everything I want him to do.' Acts 13:22 What a powerful compliment God gave David! Angela shares insights into David's heart through her meditative journal of Psalm 110 and inspires the reader to emulate David in his quest for intimacy with God.

Kathleen Trock-Molhoek
Founder of Pebbles and Stones, Author of Hiding Places

His Footstool by Angela Brown explores the most quoted Old Testament passage in the New Testament: Psalms 110. Taking David's prophetic Psalm concerning Messiah's reign, Angela shows how you, as a believer in Jesus, can now experience the stunning realities of his reign. *His Footstool* spreads a banquet of blessings that are all yours in Christ Jesus. Read, taste and see how good the Lord is!

Mark Nysewander
Teaching Pastor, Riverstone Church
Author, *The Fasting Key* and *No More Spectators*

I've known Angela Brown for many years now through the ministry of The Worship Studio and it's my great pleasure to endorse her new book! I know it will encourage you on your faith journey as it did me. Do yourself a favor and put this on your must-read list this year!

Matt Tommey
Founder, The Worship Studio
Author, *Unlocking the Heart of the Artist, Crafting Your Brand* and *Creativity According to the Kingdom*

During the past five years, my wife Anita and I have come to know Angela Brown within the context of a long-term and highly effective worship and prayer gathering. She is a woman of great faith and a deep revelatory understanding of God, His Word and His ways. The book you now hold in your hands is a written testament to the clarity and depth of those revelatory understandings. His Footstool is a brightly lighted path to knowing God and understanding His ways at a level you may have never known or perhaps even imagined as possible.

Dave Duggan
Blessings2All Ministries, Inc
Kennesaw, Georgia

DEDICATION

This book is dedicated to my Word of Love family. Without your prayers, encouragement, loving correction and friendship over the years, this book would not have been possible. You have loved and supported me through many challenging seasons in my life for the last thirty years. Thank you for being the Body of Christ to me and in your realms of influence. You are a priceless treasure created in God's heart.

ACKNOWLEDGMENTS

First of all, I want to thank my husband of 47 years for his support and encouragement to finally finish this book. You are a patient soul and a wonderful partner.

Thank you Germaine Copeland for laying a firm foundation in my life from the Word of God and giving me the first opportunity to teach this message over 30 years ago.

Thank you Pat and Gene Gastineau for your wisdom, insight and encouragement to use the gifts the Lord has granted me and for your prayers and leadership for over 30 years.

Thank you Mark Nysewander, David Smith and Dave Duggan for your wisdom and godly insights as I began to put this message into words.

Thanks also to Rhonda Fleming for your expert editing skills in helping me whip this manuscript into shape and for being a patient sounding board and friend.

TABLE OF CONTENTS

PSALM 110:7

PSALM 110 CONCLUSION

NOTE FROM THE AUTHOR

The Psalms have always been a tremendous source of comfort to me during my walk with the Lord. The transparency so evident in these writings awakens in me a greater awareness of God in my times of fear, frustration, joy and sorrow.

The intimate exchange of deep devotion expressed between the writers and God greatly encourages me. Their heartfelt expressions have challenged me to become more authentic in my own communication with the Lord.

The Psalms express genuine affection between the Lord and his children. They are like a textbook of worship. They can be used to express deep feelings when you are unable to find any words of your own. They introduce a language of devotion the Lord desires to teach each one of His children. The Psalms help you experience a taste of the passion of the Lord.

You can also use the Psalms to guide you into God's presence and power. I often read one of them aloud to begin my conversations with the Lord. This practice serves as a springboard to launch me into my own words of love, worship and intercession.

Many years ago as I prayed through Psalm 110, the Holy Spirit revealed a new and profound understanding of Father God's heart and the Lordship of Jesus Christ. Even as I write this book, He continues to expand this revelation, sweeten His presence within and challenge me to pursue Him passionately.

1

Since I started studying Psalm 110, I have had opportunities to share my revelations with several groups of people. Each time I do, I realize there is a depth of revelation in this Psalm that encourages people to really explore their own intimacy with the Lord. It excites the spirit within us and opens up the realm of the prophetic with a greater depth and understanding.

In case the "prophetic realm" isn't familiar to you, here is some background. In the book of Revelation, John shares his encounter with an angel who explains prophecy to him:

Worship God! For the substance (essence) of the truth revealed by Jesus is the spirit of all prophecy [the vital breath, the inspiration of all inspired preaching and interpretations of the divine will and purpose, including both mine and yours]. Revelation 19:10b (Amplified Bible)

Prophecy is simply the word of Jesus concerning the truth He is willing to share with any of us who will stop and listen for His voice. Sometimes He shares these truths with us even when we are not trying to hear.

The apostle Paul encouraged the Corinthian church by telling them to:

Eagerly pursue and seek to acquire [this] love [make it your aim, your great quest]; and earnestly desire and cultivate the spiritual endowments (gifts), especially that you may prophesy (interpret the divine will and purpose in inspired preaching and teaching)...the one who prophesies [who interprets the divine will and purpose in inspired preaching and teaching] speaks to men for their upbuilding and constructive spiritual progress and encouragement and consolation. 1 Corinthians 14:1, 3 (Amplified Bible)

Father God wants all of His children to desire and cultivate prophetic ability so they can receive His words of truth for their upbuilding and spiritual progress and encouragement and consolation. Learning about and participating in the realm of the prophetic is not some fantasy exercise relegated to a chosen few. It is simply the way you receive and understand truths that will prepare you for the future and encourage you in your daily life. God desires to give you this understanding and ability so you can receive His love in greater depth and share it with others the way He would.

So my goal in writing this book is to encourage you with a new understanding of ways the Lord wants to visit us with His intimate love and draw us upward into the realm of heaven. In that place of intimacy we can experience His perspective on life in His kingdom and the destiny we have been given as sons and daughters of the Most High God. Then, we can exhibit His heart through our lives here on earth.

INTRODUCTION

In August of 1969, I watched my husband go off to war in Viet Nam. It was agonizing. As hard as it was for me, a young wife, to watch my soldier husband leave that day, I know his parents felt something much deeper in their souls than I possibly could.

You see, my husband was the youngest of four sons and the third one to leave and serve in the Armed Forces of our country. The others were now home safe and sound. But I know his parents wondered if he would ever come back home—and if he did, would he come back whole. Although he was only in Viet Nam for a year, every day we spent without him was stressful and anxious.

The day my husband arrived back in the States, he and I drove to his parents' home. They were waiting on the front porch with a huge "Welcome Home" banner draped above the front steps. They stood there beaming, with smiles and tears. It was a joyous and emotional homecoming. But it was also a very intimate occasion. There were no strangers invited to watch our reunion and to observe our displays of deep emotions. It was a private and personal event for us.

On that day, we all experienced such a feeling of relief and completion. My husband had carried out his assignment and now we could all sit back and once again enjoy his presence without fear and anxiety. We could once again experience his smile and enjoy his touch and share our love for each other in person. It was a monumental day in all our lives.

Psalm 110 is a picture of the divine reunion between the God of the Universe and His Son, Jesus Christ, upon His return from earth where He suffered, died and rose again. I don't believe any of us can imagine the depth of love and the amount of celebration that took place in heaven as Father and Son were reunited after Jesus's death on the cross, His agony in the grave and His resurrection victory. Yes, all of heaven was rejoicing as the angels watched, in amazement and wonder, this glorious reunion of Father and Son.

What is even more astounding to me is that the God of the Universe invited a simple man who grew up as a humble shepherd to witness this divine reunion. As Jesus again took His place on the Throne of Heaven after His death and resurrection, the Father mysteriously shared—with a mere human—this intimate exchange with His Son. By allowing David to be privy to this powerful scene, the Father displayed His deep desire and intent to involve mankind in all of His miraculous plans to redeem His fallen creation and to teach them about intimate relationship. David must have had a special bond with Father God. Why else would he have been invited to witness this intimate event?

Our God is real in every sense of the word. And He longs for people who will live boldly and honestly before Him as David did. God is never shocked by our words or actions. He sees us as we really are. And He longs to show us who He really is. He desires to reveal to us who He created us to be on earth and in the heavenly realm.

Psalm 110 shows us that the only way we can be transformed into the likeness of Father God is through sincere communication and unreserved devotion. Genuine expression of the soul rarely takes place between mere acquaintances. True intimacy is reserved for trusted relationships.

Another amazing revelation I discovered in Psalm 110 is the abundance of power and authority God entrusts to those who know Him intimately. He has called us to be extensions of His grace and power in the earth. He desires that we, who were once strangers and even enemies, will become passionate volunteers displaying His character, compassion and power through our lives. He equips us to walk among humanity as His sons and daughters, created in the image and likeness of His Son, Jesus Christ.

I also see in Psalm 110 God's amazing plan to use the enemies of Christ to usher in the triumphant second coming of Jesus to earth. The full redemption of God's creation and the climax of the ages will become reality when the Head, Jesus Christ, is fully exalted by and manifested through His body, the Church.

Please understand that I am not a Hebrew or Greek scholar nor am I a theologian. I am a simple woman who loves to study the Word of God and believes Holy Spirit grants revelation to every person who takes time to read and pray from the written Word. The things I have learned from this psalm have challenged and encouraged me for many years.

Some of you may find these revelations to be new and different from your present understanding of God. Some of you may see far deeper revelations than I have expressed in my interpretation of Psalm 110. No matter how you perceive what I have written, the truth is we have only scratched the surface of God's desire to be one with those who know Him as Lord. My hope is for you to be encouraged and challenged to go deeper in relationship with the Living Word, Jesus Christ, as you read and meditate upon His written word.

God intended from the beginning of time to redeem His lost creation and establish His kingdom on earth as it is in heaven. You and I have a vital part in His amazing redemption plan. Jesus is waiting for us to be vitally united with Him in intimacy and power. He lifts His head triumphantly as we display His victory on the cross as citizens of His kingdom on earth.

What a calling! What a destiny He has designed for each of us! Join me as we explore some of the wonderful treasures of Psalm 110. May you experience His presence and His power to passionately live out your destiny as a child of the Father, follower of His Son, Jesus Christ, and student of our Teacher, the Holy Spirit.

OVERVIEW

You prepare a table before me in the
presence of my enemies.
You anoint my head with oil;
My [brimming] cup runs over.

Psalm 23:5 (Amplified Bible)

CHAPTER ONE

THE CRUCIBLE OF PREPARATION

It is believed that the author of Psalm 110 was David, king of Israel. David wrote many hundreds of psalms and put a whole company of worshippers in place in the tabernacle to worship Jehovah twenty-four hours a day. Many of his psalms were quite prophetic in nature and pointed to the coming Messiah. Psalm 110 is one of those psalms.

As king, David led Israel into a place of prominence and prosperity that lasted for generations. His leadership skills and visionary ability were phenomenal. He left a great legacy for his own bloodline and for all who would choose to worship His God.

We are going to examine this life that God ordained and prepared to receive and deliver His redemptive vision for the generations that followed. There is much to learn from David's growth and development in the presence of His God.

David, the son of Jesse, was very young when he began to experience God's greatness. While he was no different than other boys of that time and culture, David was drawn into a unique place in God's heart. In that extraordinary place, he developed a prophetic voice that would enable him to lead Israel and declare Jehovah's salvation plan for the human race. Can you imagine yourself at the age of 14 spending most of your day communing with God? Can you imagine a 14-year-old in today's culture spending that much time alone with God? Most youth today are so busy with homework, sports, video games, texting, social events and even church activities that they hardly have time for their families—much less quality time to spend with God figuring out the life they were created to live. And there are many teens today living in a dangerous atmosphere of abuse or neglect who spend their time just trying to survive.

Now, try to imagine yourself as David at age 14. You live your life alone in your father's fields. Your father's sheep are your only companions. You care for the sheep. They are your family's livelihood. Your job is to daily find fresh pastures and clean water. You must make sure the sheep are healthy and safe.

You must also, without anyone else's help, defend the sheep from predators. Lions and bears occasionally stalk the flock, attempting to steal away the helpless lambs. A slingshot and a knife are your only weapons. Your seven brothers gloriously serve in your country's great army, but you fight alone, using primitive tools with little recognition of your service. There is no glory in the pastures. There are no comrades to share your tales of battle.

Night and day you have endless hours to ponder the creation around you. You rehearse the stories of your family's heritage and their faith. These stories keep you vitally linked to your family and their God.

Music is your leisure pastime. You sing and play your lyre to calm the sheep and entertain yourself in the solitude. As you practice your music, new melodies and lyrics form in your heart. You feel the pleasure and presence of the God of your family. He pursues your attention and woos your affection as a personal friend.

Gradually, your mind is captured by Him and filled with His words. He becomes your strength in battle, your deliverer from loneliness and your joy in the midst of sorrow. Your heart becomes centered on His words and His presence. Contentment floods your life of simplicity and solitude.

Now, imagine how you might feel when you are suddenly called to your father's house. You learn that a prophet of God has come to anoint you (See 1 Samuel 16). As the prophet pours oil over your head, you are abruptly thrust into another dimension. The Spirit of the Living God comes to rest upon your life. You sense that something is different. What is the reason for this anointing by the prophet? How will it affect your future? No one could ever guess that an adolescent shepherd would be called to become the next king of Israel.

Soon doors of favor are opened to you. You are called to the king's palace to play your lyre and sing your songs for the tormented king. Others have attempted to soothe the soul of this anguished ruler, but with no results. Now, they are looking to you to bring solace and comfort to the leader of your country.

All you have to give your troubled king are words and melodies created from the cries of your own heart in the midst of a lonely country field. With fear and trembling, you sing and play with all your might. Strangely, the music seems to have great power. The restless, tormented ruler is calmed like one of your sheep in the dark hours of the night. His countenance is changed and peace permeates the atmosphere of his royal palace. And you have been plucked from the solitude and simplicity of the sheep fields and planted in the extravagant realm of royal society.

Your God has done it again. He has brought you into an impossible situation. He has given you the power to stand before a king. Demons flee like wounded animals in the presence of your anointed melodies. Your favor with the king is secured. You have moved from the pasture to the palace, from obscurity to notoriety. Only your God could do such a thing.

The Product of Preparation

The lonely sheep-tending life of young David was his crucible of preparation. He was the youngest of his seven brothers. He began as a shepherd, learned to be a warrior and transformed into a charismatic poet and musician. He grew courageous and acquired wisdom in the company of dumb animals. He was trained by Jehovah God to be ready to step into a place of royalty and riches.

As king of Israel, David flourished in influence. The stories of his tragedies and triumphs still inspire those who read them today. David was a mighty warrior, a wise king and a triumphant leader. But his intimate relationship with Jehovah God created in him the heart of a prophetic poet.

In the secret place, alone in the pastures, the heart of young David was knit together with the heart of His God. The triune Creator of the universe chose this simple man with a heart of worship to become His witness to an amazing, futuristic event. It was the event that would change the fabric of God's ultimate creation from fallen to forgiven.

David was chosen to use his inspired words to unveil the resurrection reunion between the Joy of Heaven and His Father God. The Father of mankind enabled this man who was once a common shepherd to become a king and record His legacy of unconditional love for the generations yet to come.

In several of the psalms David wrote, he recorded words that clearly speak of the crucifixion, death and resurrection of the Lord Jesus Christ:

15

My God, my God, why have You forsaken me?...I am poured out like water, and all my bones are out of joint...They part my clothing among them and cast lots for my raiment...Psalm 22:1, 14, 18 (Amplified Bible)

Yes, though I walk through the [deep, sunless] valley of the shadow of death, I will fear or dread no evil, for You are with me...You prepare a table before me in the presence of my enemies. You anoint my head with oil...Psalm 23:4-5 (Amplified Bible)

Lift up your heads, O you gates; and be lifted up, you age-abiding doors, that the King of glory may come in...Who is [He then] this King of glory? The Lord of Hosts, He is the King of glory.   Psalm 24:7-10 (Amplified Bible)

Psalm 110 is another example of the exceptional prophetic insight David was given. His daily experiences, in secret before the Lord, became a strange crucible of preparation, enabling him to hear and observe the events he recorded in all these psalms. I am convinced that Psalm 110 contains revelation far beyond David's personal knowledge of God.

The Father chose David to receive and record this information, preserving it for all future generations. Through this psalm, God's grace reaches into eternity and draws us all back in time to this mysterious encounter between a man and his Creator.

Why David?

God's sovereign choice of an insignificant shepherd boy seems ridiculous. But when viewed from the perspective of God's amazing grace, it makes perfect sense. What did David have that suited him to receive prophetic revelation? I believe it was one simple element—availability.

David made himself available to God through praise, worship and time spent meditating on God and His creation. He had real responsibilities that could have consumed his thoughts. He could have spent his time resenting his lot in life and wallowing in self-pity. Instead, David dreamed. He let his imagination take him into the presence of the Living God for a personal encounter. He looked up to his Creator and followed Him into a place bigger than life. He became a sheep in the heavenly fields of the Great Shepherd.

David could have run from this sovereign opportunity to discover his God. But he didn't. Today you have that same choice. You can enjoy the vision of David's personal encounter and be encouraged to enter into your own adventure with God. Or you can settle for a less-than life, one without opportunities to experience the unseen realms of glory and grace prepared especially for you. If you don't settle, you could receive an earth-changing revelation, given by God, for all generations. Are you making yourself available?

In this book, I have attempted to share my present understanding of Psalm 110. It is just a starting place for us to delve deeper into the vast revelation to be found in this psalm. I pray it will encourage you to go deeper into relationship with the Father, His Son and His Holy Spirit. May you discover a fresh new view of our extraordinary God. Let His unique expression of love in Christ Jesus draw you into a vibrant intimacy with your Creator and King. In that intimacy, may you discover the passionate, powerful person God created *you* to be.

ONLY GOD

Only God can make a boy into a king.

Only God can cause a fool to be wise.

Only God can lift a thought above the earth.

Only God can make a dream into a truth.

Only God can cause a rebel to bow at His throne.

Only God can transform a heart into His footstool.

Questions for Reflection:

Who does most of the talking when you spend time with the Lord? *me*

How often do you make yourself available to listen to the Lord? *not enough*

What are some ways you could increase your availability to hear from the Lord?

by reading His Word – especially the Psalms

PSALM 110:1

The Lord said to my Lord, "Sit at My right hand,
till I make Your enemies Your footstool."

The word of God to my Lord:
"Sit alongside me here on My
throne until I make your
enemies a stool for your feet."
(The Message)

CHAPTER TWO

UNFOLDING REVELATION

The Lord has given everyone an imagination. You can see imagination working quite vividly as you watch small children at play. They easily step into their imaginary realms, talking and interacting with unseen characters as if they were standing right next to them. They seem to perceive sounds, colors and shapes that are invisible to most adults. Using their imagination comes naturally with no instructions or program to follow. They just step into a place of interest and let their imagination guide them into new discoveries and adventures.

Sadly, much of our God-given imagination is squelched by our systems of education and our experiences in the visible world even before we enter adolescence. We begin to believe that imagination is just a childish tool that should be pushed aside as we grow into adulthood. And we, unfortunately, buy in to the lie that imagination is designed for children and has no place in the lives of mature men and women.

God designed the imagination. He created humans with this ability in order to receive revelations to ponder, practice or pass on to others. Your imagination should be maturing as your body and mind matures. You should be growing in the skill of using your imagination to interact with the God of the universe so you can more readily understand His ways of creativity and relationship. A healthy and surrendered imagination is a valuable asset to possess in life.

Every great invention began in someone's imagination. If the inventor had not taken the time to use his imagination to receive pictures and perceptions, he would not have been able to form and produce something that would benefit his own life and the lives of those around him. Think of all the breakthroughs in science, medicine, travel and technology that we enjoy every day. All those wonderful tools began with someone dreaming and imagining the possibility of their existence.

You need your imagination to be in full working order! The Holy Spirit works through imagination to bring divinely inspired dreams, thoughts and revelations. A vivid and godly imagination is an essential tool for divine dreamers. Joel, an Old Testament prophet, prophesied God's desire to use the imagination of men and women to receive His counsel, visions and dreams for the days we live in. And Peter reminded God's people again of His intentions on the day of Pentecost.

And it shall come to pass in the last days, God declares, That I will pour out of My Spirit upon all mankind, and your sons and daughters shall prophesy [telling forth the divine counsels] and your young men shall see vi-

sions (divinely granted appearances), and your old men shall dream [divinely suggested] dreams. Acts 2:17 (Amplified Bible)

As we study Psalm 110, remember, you are equipped by the Holy Spirit to use your imagination. Like David, you can receive God's counsel, visions and dreams for your life and the lives of others.

David Dreamed

David dreamed, diligently exercising and developing his imagination. The many hours he spent alone with God in the pastures of Israel became a training ground for receiving and imparting revelations. Throughout David's life, the Lord gave him revelations to release into the earth.

In the first verse of Psalm 110, David unfolds a prophetic revelation he experienced. He reveals an awesome conversation between the God David knew as Jehovah (self-existent or eternal) and someone David referred to as his lord (Adon-sovereign, master, owner). Many Bible commentaries reveal this passage points ahead to the Messiah. David only knew his God was addressing another lord. The form of the word "lord" that David used here was also used when attached to an earthly ruler's name.

David recognized this lord as his own sovereign ruler. Did he actually realize Adon was the Messiah the prophets predicted? We don't really know. David may have thought of Him as only another man with political authority. Understanding this Adon to be the actual Son of God was probably not a part of his spiritual knowledge. David only understood that Jehovah was inviting Adon to sit at the favored place of His right hand on the very Throne of Heaven.

Whether David realized it or not, he was witness to the history-changing event yet to occur in the realm of earth's time zone. David was witnessing the homecoming of Jesus into the presence of His Father after His death on the cross and His resurrection from the grave. It's hard for us to imagine being privy to such an awesome event before it even took place.

26

David heard, with his spiritual ears, the awe-inspiring invitation of Jehovah God to His beloved only Son to join Him on His throne once again. The throne was where the awesome trio of Father, Son and Holy Spirit conceived and created the heavens, the earth and the man they formed into their image.

God said, "Let Us make mankind in Our image, after Our likeness..." Genesis 1:26

In the beginning was the Word and the Word was with God, and the Word was God Himself. He was present originally with God. All things were made and came into existence through Him; and without Him was not even one thing made that has come into being. John 1:1-3

Why would the Living God share such a defining moment in time with a mere human being? David was not a perfect man by any means. As an adult, he even conspired to murder so he could have another man's wife. God knew David's weaknesses before he ever displayed them. His decision to share this event with David was not based on perfect performance. The Father's confidence was in the deep deposit of divine love He had invested in David's heart.

Years earlier God saw the heart of David as a youth in the sheepfolds. He enjoyed his unbridled devotion. The Father knew He had captured David's heart. He knew David would never be satisfied with anything less than real intimacy with his God.

When the prophet Samuel questioned God's rejection of David's oldest brother as king of Israel, the Lord replied,

> *Look not on his appearance or at the height of his stature, for I have rejected him. For the Lord sees not as man sees; for man looks on the outward appearance, but the Lord looks on the heart. 1 Samuel 16:7*

The Lord chose David instead of his seven older brothers. He knew David's heart was secure in the intimate love and holy presence of his God. David had learned to hear Jehovah's heartbeat and was willing to follow His lead.

In the quietness of solitude, David became a lover of God. He was a willing vessel to receive the revelations of the Father and meditate on them. They became reality to David. He set many of these revelations to music and rehearsed them often.

Throughout David's life, this particular psalm became a prophetic declaration to usher God's desire into the earth realm. The intimate exchanges of adoration and assurance between David and God paved a way for prophetic revelation to be imparted to his flawed human heart. The Father trusted David to watch, listen and record this reunion and the divine promise He was making to His Son.

This deep intimacy between God and David has intrigued me for years. I now realize our Father is not afraid to share His own desires with imperfect people—people like you and me. Any one of us can become a chosen vessel to receive and declare the promises of God.

The Divine Promise

The words of the Father were emphatic as He invited Jesus to sit at His right hand until He made the Lord's enemies His footstool. Can you imagine the exuberant passion overflowing from the Father's heart toward His Son and into David's ears? The Father was promising Jesus a total and final victory over all His enemies.

The force of God's promise was made with all the love and devotion shared among Father, Son and Holy Spirit. In perfect unity they conceived and designed the awesome plan of salvation for mankind and the restoration of earth into the Kingdom of God. Suddenly, all of earth's history shifted through this mighty, sovereign promise of victory.

As Jesus rose from the dead and took His seat next to Father God, heaven rejoiced, hell shook and earth groaned in expectation of the final triumph. All creation would bow before His throne. As the Father's divine promise to Jesus exploded into the atmosphere, David was given an awesome revelation of the magnitude of Jehovah's heart.

The apostle Paul wrote about this desire in the heart of the Father for His Son to be honored and exalted above all others:

And being found in appearance as a man, He humbled Himself and became obedient to the point of death, even the death of the cross. Therefore God also has highly exalted Him and given Him the name which is above every name, that at the name of Jesus every knee should bow, of those in heaven and of those on earth, and of those under the earth, and that every tongue should confess that Jesus Christ is Lord, to the glory of God the Father. Philippians 2:8-11

It is amazing to think about David being swept up into this reunion of Almighty God and His Son. Imagine being able to witness and record a divine proclamation that would change heaven and earth forever!

As a king, David understood the authority and integrity contained in this divine promise to Jesus. Jehovah God invited Jesus to sit at His right hand. This position beside the God of creation would be one of reigning. Very few were given such a place in David's experience. Kingship was a sovereign, solitary position. As David witnessed this invitation, he acknowledged Jesus as his own sovereign ruler by calling Him Adon.

Jesus had completed His part of the divine salvation plan to reveal the heart of the Father to His people. He came to earth in the form of an innocent child with the same human nature as mankind (John 1:14, Hebrews 2:14, 17). But He revealed, even as a child, His relationship of oneness with Jehovah (Luke 2:41-51). All throughout His life on earth, He displayed the heart of the Father so all people could see the goodness and glory of God (John 14:8-9, John 17:4). He paid the price on the cross for our redemption so we could be ushered into the Father's presence (Romans 3:22-26; 5:8-11). And through faith in Jesus Christ as the Son of God, all men can be justified and accepted by God and saved from the penalty of sin (Romans 10:8-13).

What is the penalty of sin? Romans 6:23 (Amplified Bible) answers that question:

30

For the wages which sin pays is death, but the [bounti-ful] free gift of God is eternal life through (in union with) Jesus Christ our Lord. (emphasis mine)

Sin brings death into the life of mankind but **union with Christ** brings eternal life. This reunion between Father and Son was the picture of relationship with mankind being restored. Jesus came back to the Father with a resurrected human body. He is a man seated with God on His heavenly throne. There is no separation between Jesus and the Father anymore. He is fully alive and fully present with the Father. He defeated death and is restored to relationship with the Father just like He had from the beginning—eternal life!

So, death and separation from the Father (the wages of sin) is cancelled through the death and resurrection of the Son of God. Now, the Father would complete His salvation plan by making all of the Lord's enemies become a footstool for His feet.

Even if David did not realize this Adon was God's own Son, he did understand the authority that God's word carried. He knew this promise was sure to be fulfilled because God's word was trustworthy. His word would accomplish what He pleased. This divine promise was backed by the divine guarantee of the Most Holy Father to His Most Holy Son. David knew God would fulfill this promise because He had fulfilled the promise He made to David.

Therefore all the elders of Israel came to the king at Hebron...and they anointed David king over Israel, according to the word of the Lord by Samuel.
1Chronicles 11:3

31

Enemies Revealed

The concept of changing enemies into a footstool is a strange idea. In David's time, as someone approached the king, he honored the king's authority by bowing at his feet. Then he waited until permission was given to rise and address the king.

It is hard for those born into a democratic society to understand this expression of honor. We tend to see all men as equal, often neglecting to honor authority. Too many times we see authority as oppressive rather than worthy of respect. Misuse of authority and personal rights has made us leery of that kind of submission. But David, as king of Israel, had great understanding of royal protocol. He was accustomed to seeing enemies bow at his own throne.

Who does God consider to be the enemies of Jesus? According to Strong's concordance, the Hebrew word for **enemy** in verse 1 means an adversary or foe.[1] Webster's dictionary defines an adversary as "one that contends with, opposes or resists."[2]

It is clear that Satan definitely contends with the Lord and is His ultimate opponent. Men and women who have refused to recognize and worship Jesus as the Savior and Lord of their lives could also be considered enemies of the King.

Paul wrote to the New Testament church in Rome about another enemy of God:

For those who live according to the flesh set their minds on the things of the flesh, but those who live according to the Spirit, the things of the Spirit. For to be carnally minded is death, but to be spiritually minded is life and peace. Because the carnal mind is enmity against God; for it is not subject to the law of God, nor indeed can be. So then, those who are in the flesh cannot please God. Romans 8:5-8

This mind of the flesh is possibly the most diabolical enemy of the Lord. Even after salvation, believers still have to deal with this enemy of God. He often uses the cloak of religion and goodness to hide his selfish motives. This enemy can hide for years without detection. He can live in hidden places of the heart. He resists the movement of the Holy Spirit and goes to great lengths to stay undetected. Pride and fear will keep this enemy hidden well. The only way to deal with him is to repent—agree with God!

I was shocked when I first realized I was allowing God's enemies to remain in my heart. But all of us fall short of the glory of God, even after our experience of salvation. 1 John 1:9-10 confirms this realization:

If we confess our sins, He is faithful and just to forgive us our sins and to cleanse us from all unrighteousness. If we say that we have not sinned, we make Him a liar, and His word is not in us.

Our Father God has graciously provided this door of confession and repentance as the way to stay vitally covered in His righteousness. You have no righteousness of your own. Righteousness is the free gift of God, the Father, through faith in Jesus Christ, the Son. Sin separates you from His righteousness and keeps you from receiving the blessings of sonship. (Remember death is the result of sin, but eternal life is the result of union with Christ—Romans 6:23.) The absence of confession and cleansing is the one thing that enables the enemy of God to remain in your heart to cut off the blessing of union with Christ.

Ignorance of God's word and passivity will hold you captive to the habit of sin. You must pursue His truth concerning righteousness as you would pursue water to quench your thirst. Constant communion with the Living God through His word, prayer and the help of the Holy Spirit opens up expanding revelation you need to identify the enemies of God that may be hiding in your mind, will or emotions. God desires to fully possess the throne of your heart so He can bless you with righteousness, peace and joy.

But whoever keeps His word, truly the love of God is perfected in him. By this we know that we are in Him. He who says he abides in Him ought himself also to walk just as He walked. 1 John 2:5-6

God is serious about ruling and reigning in your life because He knows you need Him. You are not capable of righteously reigning over any part of your life without God-given revelation. You must continually focus on Him as King on the throne of your heart. Without this understanding, your unrenewed mind can drift back into the old habits of self-centered living. It is common to hold onto familiar patterns of behavior excusing them as a part of your personality. However, they are acts of aggression toward God and His kingdom purposes for your life.

Understand this about your Father, God—He is for you and not against you! He gave His all to make a way for you to be present with Him through the cleansing blood of Jesus Christ. His desire is to lift the veil off of the dark places of your soul to free you of oppressive habits and beliefs that cut off His abundance of blessings. He desires for you to fully possess your destiny to be formed into His image for the glory of God and the good of His kingdom.

As a child of God, saved by the blood of Jesus, old behaviors are to pass away and new ones are to take their place. You are created to act like your Father God through the power of Christ living in you.

Therefore, if anyone is in Christ, he is a new creation; old things have passed away; behold, all things have become new.... For He made Him who knew no sin to be sin for us, that we might become the righteousness of God in Him. 2 Corinthians 5:17-21

The only way new life can be fully formed in you is to humbly realize Jesus has gained the right to rule your life. He paid the price for your reconciliation with Father God. His blood cleanses you from the effects of the sin nature, which ruled before He became your Savior. The prayer of salvation is only the starting point of a life-long practice of bowing at His footstool and following His lead.

By allowing the Holy Spirit to open up the word of God to you through prayer and study, you begin to live your life as your were created to live it—as a cherished son or daughter.

For all who are led by the Spirit of God are sons of God. Romans 8:14

35

A New Way of Freedom

Being rescued from the grip of sin is a joyous experience when you realize the wages of sin is death. On the other hand, giving up the right to rule your own life can be scary. Isn't freedom to make your own life choices the ultimate style of living? Exactly! And this is what God gave you when He sent Jesus to die on the cross. He opened up a way of freedom that previously did not exist.

Before the cross, man failed to choose righteously. Adam and Eve blew that test. Mankind cannot discern what is really good without the help of the One who is truly good. God created you and He is the only one who knows how you should live. He alone knows what gifts, talents and destiny you were created to display through your life. He is the only one who really knows how you can flourish. He is the one who uniquely designed you to live a creative and productive life reflecting His greatness, goodness and pleasure.

God, who is rich in mercy, because of His great love with which He loved us, even when we were dead in trespasses, made us alive together with Christ and raised us up together, and made us sit together in the heavenly places in Christ Jesus, that in the ages to come He might show the exceeding riches of His grace in His kindness toward us in Christ Jesus. Ephesians 2:4-7

Remembering the gift of grace you receive by faith in Jesus makes it easier to submit fully to God's desire to rule your life. When you let God control every area of your life, He can fully restore you to the original purpose He had in mind at the time of your creation.

*So God created man in His own image, in the image
and likeness of God He created him; male and female
He created them. And God blessed them and said to
them, Be fruitful, multiply, and fill the earth, and subdue it [using all its vast resources in the service of God
and man]; and have dominion over the fish of the sea,
the birds of the air, and over every living creature that
moves upon the earth. Genesis 1:27-28 (Amplified Bible)*

God's original intent was for man to carry His authority and creativity throughout the earth, reflecting His nature
and character. Today, His desire for you is the same. He delights in watching you take up His mantle of authority as He
watchfully rests within your midst. You can learn and enjoy
the rewards of creative power and use it to maintain and multiply life in the earth.

The Lord taught the children of Israel how they could
possess the land of their enemies through their obedience to
Him:

*For if you diligently keep all this commandment which I
command you to do, to love the Lord your God, to walk
in all His ways, and cleave to Him—the Lord will drive
out all these nations before you, and you shall dispos-
sess nations greater and mightier than you. Every place
upon which the sole of your foot shall tread shall be
yours...Deuteronomy 11:22-24*

The word **foot**[3] in this passage, and many others like
it, can be translated as "possession." By placing their feet in a
territory, in obedience to His instructions, they took possession of the land they walked on through His power.

As you worship and follow Him, the Lord walks into the soil of your life removing His enemies hidden within your heart. Therefore, every nook and cranny of your heart becomes the resting place for His power and authority! Then, as you walk throughout the earth in obedience to His plans, you can take possession of the land in your heart that those enemies once controlled—expanding His Kingdom on earth.

Hidden Enemies in the Heart

As Jesus began to gather disciples during His three years of ministry, most of the Pharisees could not see Him for who He actually was. They stood against Him as an enemy. The disciples of Jesus did not always follow the rules and traditions prescribed by these religious leaders. Jesus began to unravel the religious threads that prevented people from really knowing the heart of God. The Pharisees taught that ritual and tradition would make men holy. Jesus taught relationship with God would make men holy.

> *Do you not yet understand that whatever enters the mouth goes into the stomach and is eliminated? But those things which proceed out of the mouth come from the heart, and they defile a man. For out of the heart proceed evil thoughts, murders, adulteries, fornications, thefts, false witness, blasphemies. These are the things which defile a man, but to eat with unwashed hands does not defile a man. Matthew 15:17-20*

In this passage, the heart of a man refers to his mind, will and emotions. When you ask Jesus to be your Savior and Lord, the Holy Spirit miraculously brings to life the spirit within you that was dead with the nature of sin. Your spirit is immediately brought to life with the nature of Christ. You are then enabled to live in the light of God's righteousness and holiness. Your spirit becomes holy as He is holy, having the same inherent nature as Christ.

But your heart (mind, will and emotions) is blinded to the identity of the enemies of God until the Living Word (Jesus) slowly and patiently shines the light of revelation to uncover them. The discovery of evil residing in your heart is

39

the first step to freedom from the bondage of your old sin nature. The choice between darkness (sin) and light (righteousness) is presented by the Holy Spirit. Then, you can repent for living in the darkness of that enemy. By asking the Lord to remove His enemy from your heart, you welcome Him to dwell in the place where the enemy was hiding.

Where darkness and evil once prevailed and pushed you, Jesus will lead and guide you. When you choose His way of living, you are given the power to walk out of the prison of darkness into the freedom and everlasting light of His love.

Repentance becomes the highway to a holy lifestyle. Every step you take down this highway opens up new places in your heart for the Lord to rest within you with fresh grace and overcoming power.

When you give up the practices of the enemy of God, the enemy loses ground and the Lord can move into that place in your heart. That place in your heart is no longer a hiding place for the enemy of God. Instead, it becomes a footstool for God's presence and power—a resting place for His nature to dwell.

What better destiny could you ask for than to become a place for God's glory to live?

PRAYER

Lord, thank you for giving me an imagination designed to be used for Your glory. I ask for the awakening of my imagination to visualize, dream and receive Your divine counsel. Give me courage to allow you to root out Your enemies within my heart. Make me a resting place for Your great power and mercy, a footstool for Your presence. In the mighty name of Jesus, Amen.

41

Questions for Reflection:

How do you imagine God the Father, Jesus and Holy Spirit when you pray?

What ideas or visions have you received that you think could help change the world around you?

What enemies of God do you think might still be hiding in your heart?

CHAPTER THREE

EMBRACING THE FOOTSTOOL

The idea of becoming the resting place of God is fascinating. God's plan to make this idea a reality in us is simple. He wants to replace the old lies we have believed with His glorious truth. When we begin to live by His truth, the Lord has a larger resting place—free of His enemies—within our heart. However, this simple process is not always an easy one.

Have you ever had to replace an older favorite appliance or maybe a vehicle you have driven for many years? Sometimes it's hard to let go of that familiar way of functioning in your kitchen or driving down the road. You want to hang on to it because you know how to operate it without even thinking. It feels comfortable. It has become an old friend.

But then you realize it may be dangerous to operate. That old appliance could experience an electrical short and cause a fire. Or the brakes on that old truck might give out and cause you to have a wreck. You can rationalize it, but letting go of that familiar friend is still hard to do. It means you will have to learn to operate in new ways and upgrade your patterns of behavior.

As you begin to allow Holy Spirit to upgrade your relationship with God, you can run into these same feelings of uneasiness about letting go of familiar patterns of behavior. You cannot change your heart (mind, will and emotions) through rationalization and behavior modification. The only way to replace these sinful but familiar patterns of behavior is to exercise the gift of repentance. Father God is eager to give you this gift to make a bigger resting place for His presence within you.

Let God arise, let His enemies be scattered...Psalm 68:1a

Touchy Subject

For the next few pages, I am going to talk about repentance. The world and many churchgoers avoid this subject because it makes some people uncomfortable. The word repentance often brings up feelings of shame, regret and heaviness. Yes, we need to be saddened at the presence of sin in our lives. However, God's conviction does not bring shame. God's goal is to lead us to repentance, which allows Him to continue to transform us into all He originally created us to be—children living in His likeness!

So, I want to encourage you to read this chapter about embracing the footstool of God as a move further into your eternal destiny as a child of God and a disciple of Jesus Christ. You were created for the Kingdom of God, for the display of His glory and for His pleasure. Without true repentance, you will miss out on your intended destiny on this earth and will lose the treasure of more joy in His eternal presence.

> *Therefore let us go on and get past the elementary stage in the teachings and doctrine of Christ (the Messiah), advancing steadily toward the completeness and perfection that belong to spiritual maturity. Let us not again be laying the foundation of repentance and abandonment of dead works (dead formalism) and of the faith [by which you turned] to God...Hebrews 6:1*

Repentance is really a foundation stone in the building up of your new life in Christ. Without a firm foundation based on a solid understanding of the need and process of repentance, you cannot fully move on to the mature things of living and operating as citizens of the Kingdom of God. That is your new identity in Christ—not your earthly national, ethnic or family identity. As a Christian, you are first and foremost a child of God and a citizen of His kingdom designed to carry responsibility and authority from that kingdom to this earth.

The apostle, Paul, adamantly exhorted the Romans concerning the kindness of God connected with the act of repentance:

> *Or are you [so blind as to] trifle with and presume upon and despise and underestimate the wealth of His kindness and forbearance and longsuffering patience? Are you unmindful or actually ignorant [of the fact] that God's kindness is intended to lead you to repent (to change your mind and inner man to accept God's will)? Romans 2:4 (Amplified Bible)*

True repentance requires a change in mindset and position in order to be willing and ready to accept the will of God. Your Father's desire is for you to be firm and secure in the way of repentance and the necessity for you to exercise this gift so that you might grow up and become all He created you to be in relationship and responsibility with Him and His kingdom. Truly, His kindness never gives up on you and continually pursues you with His truth and righteousness.

Identifying Sin

We have a tendency to think of sin as the obvious bad habits like lying, cheating, stealing, swearing and addictive behaviors. Those sins may need to be addressed in your life, but sin is also deceptive in nature and often masquerades as good works. Even the good works you do can be sinful if the Lord has called you to do something different. The act in itself may not be a sin, but your choice to do it rather than what God is calling you to do is sinful. His plans for you are very specific at times and fit into a much bigger picture than your own personal satisfaction.

You may enjoy an activity that is not evil because it makes you feel good about yourself. But the Lord may call you to something totally different. And His will for you may not produce immediate evidence of its eternal value to others, but may instead have long reaching effects in the lives of other people or even an entire generation.

Noah is a great example of this type of choice. Noah looked like a fool to those in his town. They mocked him and his work. But he saved a remnant of humanity by his obedience. What if Noah had chosen instead to feed the poor or build a monument to God? Then, all mankind would have been destroyed and where would we be today?

Yes, feeding the poor is a calling from God, but it may not be what He has called you to devote your life to. That doesn't mean it is a lesser call for those who hear His voice clearly to do so. But you can't hide in the soup kitchen if He has called you to the prayer room, the boardroom or a prison ministry. Whatever God has designed you to do is what will bring Him glory and put a smile on His face when you do it!

Each person must learn to hear the voice of God and His specific call on their individual life. All Christians must lay down the good they may want to do for God's best He's calling them to do. And remember, He provides much grace to learn and discern. You may miss it from time to time. But as the truth is revealed by the Holy Spirit, you can climb back on that highway to holiness by repenting—embracing the footstool of Jesus once again. You can repent for not trusting Him—or possibly for not even listening to Him—and then accept the perfect plan He has designed for your life.

A Gift from God

Jesus made an astounding statement in response to those who could only see Him as the son of Joseph:

> *"No one can come to Me unless the Father who sent Me draws him; and I will raise him up at the last day. It is written in the prophets, 'And they shall all be taught by God.' Therefore everyone who has heard and learned from the Father comes to Me."* John 6:44-45

It is Father God who draws men and women into the revelation that Jesus is His Son and that He is the only way to eternal life. The Father gifts you with this knowledge and the ability to repent for your sins and acknowledge Jesus as your Savior. As you grow and learn to cry out to the Father to be formed into the likeness of Christ, He gifts you again with repentance for the things that hinder you from walking in the entire truth. Repentance is the gift the Father gives to His children who desire intimacy with Him and who desire His truth reigning in their lives.

Repentance is the only true way of life for the believer. Without repentance you cannot enter the kingdom of God. Then, without repentance you cannot move and grow within His kingdom. Unfortunately, repentance has become a dirty word to many people, but it is a gift from the Lord. The act of repentance is worship. It is the recognition of God's absolute power and authority. It is agreement with God about *your* life.

True repentance is heartfelt sorrow leading you to forgiveness and freedom. It is sorrow for falling short of God's glorious plan for your life. It is **not** a condemning place of hopelessness and defeat. It is **not** the continual rehearsal of

49

regrets or just saying you are sorry. True repentance will propel you into a new realization of your divine destiny. It is the vehicle to life and growth.

Just like the seed must die to produce the plant that brings forth fruit, your old way of living life must die in order for you to grow in God's grace and bring forth godly fruit—the nature of God Himself. David explained the secret joy of repentance when He wrote Psalm 32.

> *Blessed (happy, fortunate, to be envied) is he who has forgiveness of his transgression continually exercised upon him, whose sin is covered.*
>
> *Blessed (happy, fortunate, to be envied) is the man to whom the Lord imputes no iniquity and in whose spirit there is no deceit....*
>
> *For this [forgiveness] let everyone who is godly pray--Psalm 32:1-6a (Amplified Bible)*

Did you notice? It is the godly who pray this prayer! Yes, those who are seeking God with all their hearts will live a life of continual repentance as they pursue His presence. The closer you are drawn toward God, the deeper He will take you into the cleansing flow of His love. His love exposes the deceptive nature of sin so you can allow His good character to dwell in all of your heart.

> *Many are the sorrows of the wicked, but he who trusts in, relies on, and confidently leans on the Lord shall be compassed about with mercy and with loving-kindness.*
>
> *Be glad in the Lord and rejoice, you [uncompromisingly] righteous [you who are upright and in right*

standing with Him]; shout for joy, all you upright in heart! Psalm 32:10-11 (Amplified Bible)

David completed Psalm 32 with the wonderful promise of mercy, loving kindness and joy residing in the heart of the repentant soul. Many are the sorrows of those who remain in the pride and darkness of unconfessed sin. But freedom comes to the deeply repentant.

I love the way Eugene Peterson phrases Jesus words from John 6:44-45 in The Message:

The Father who sent me is in charge. He draws people to me—that's the only way you'll ever come. Only then do I do my work, putting people together, setting them on their feet, ready for the End. This is what the prophets meant when they wrote, 'And then they will all be personally taught by God.' Anyone who has spent any time at all listening to the Father, really listening and therefore learning, comes to me to be taught personally—to see it with his own eyes, hear it with his own ears, from me, since I have it firsthand from the Father.

What a glorious gift from the Father! His gift of repentance opens the door to intimacy with Jesus and a transformed life. It is available to all who will listen to and agree with God concerning sin and righteousness.

Obscure Opponent

Sin is not always obvious. It can be an obscure opponent of your new life in Christ Jesus. The life you were leading when you entered the Kingdom was bound in the grave clothes of rebellion and strife. Now the Spirit of the Lord desires to unwrap all areas of your heart and set you free to live life as Jesus did. By repenting of these obscure sins as the Holy Spirit reveals them, you embrace the footstool of God and are lifted up to a life of freedom and fullness at His right hand.

The Spirit of the Lord God is upon me, because the Lord has anointed and qualified me to preach the Gospel of good tidings to the meek, the poor, and afflicted; He has sent me to bind up and heal the brokenhearted, to proclaim liberty to the [physical and spiritual] captives and the opening of the prison and of the eyes to those who are bound.

To proclaim the acceptable year of the Lord [the year of His favor] and the day of vengeance of our God, to comfort all who mourn.

To grant [consolation and joy] to those who mourn in Zion—to give them an ornament (a garland or diadem) of beauty instead of ashes, the oil of joy instead of mourning, the garment [expressive] of praise instead of a heavy, burdened, and failing spirit—that they may be called oaks of righteousness [lofty, strong, and magnificent, distinguished for uprightness, justice and right standing with God], the planting of the Lord, that He may be glorified. Isaiah 61:1-3 (Amplified Bible)

Jesus read this passage from Isaiah in the synagogue of Nazareth at the outset of His earthly ministry. He proclaimed He had come to fulfill it (Luke 4:16-21). He is still proclaiming His anointing as Liberator today. He desires to deposit His life within every heart to set them free from the bondage of sin and the death it inflicts.

Great relief comes when hidden sin is brought into the glorious light of His love. The struggle to keep it hidden is laid aside and the warmth of His love dissolves the darkness. The Holy Spirit fills your heart with His unconditional acceptance and cleansing power. Then, you are able to move about freely in the light of His grace. You are empowered to become the person He created you to be. Great joy comes with freedom from the fear of exposure and condemnation.

Shame and fear of punishment can cause you to hide your sins. The love of Christ compels you to lay them aside and move freely into His presence. In Hebrews 12:1-2, we are encouraged to...

> *lay aside every weight, and the sin which so easily ensnares us, and let us run with endurance the race that is set before us, looking unto Jesus, the author and finisher of our faith, who for the joy that was set before Him endured the cross, despising the shame, and has sat down at the right hand of the throne of God.*

These verses depict sin as a heavy burden weighing you down so you cannot finish the race in victory. This word "weight" metaphorically means encumbrance[1]. It is a restricting weight. The weight of sin weakens and afflicts your mind, will, emotions and physical body. The only weight a disciple of Christ should be carrying is the *weight of His glory.*

> *For our light, momentary affliction (this slight distress of the passing hour) is ever more and more abundantly preparing and producing and achieving for us an ever-lasting weight of glory [beyond all measure, excessively surpassing all comparisons and all calculations, a vast and transcendent glory and blessedness never to cease!] 2 Corinthians 4:17 (Amplified Bible)*

This weight is not a burden because His strength in you empowers you to bear it. The weight of His glory is an abundant load of authority you were created to carry[2,3]. You carry it with praise and worship in your heart and on your lips. This weight of glory is often referred to as an "anointing." It enables you to carry the very presence of God Himself into the places He sends you.

Springing into Righteousness

Father God's awesome plan of redemption includes the continual washing of your soul. Through repentance you can keep enjoying open and life-giving communication with Him. His wise counsel and abundant joy continually feed those who bow at the footstool of the Lord's presence.

> *But God—so rich is He in His mercy! Because of and in order to satisfy the great and wonderful and intense love with which He loved us,*
>
> *Even when we were dead (slain) by [our own] shortcomings and trespasses, He made us alive together in fellowship and in union with Christ; [He gave us the very life of Christ Himself, the same new life with which He quickened Him, for] it is by grace (His favor and mercy which you did not deserve) that you are saved (delivered from judgment and made partakers of Christ's salvation),*
>
> *And He raised us up together with Him and made us sit down together [giving us joint seating with Him] in the heavenly sphere [by virtue of our being] in Christ Jesus (the Messiah, the Anointed One). Ephesians 2:4-6 (Amplified Bible)*

This scripture came alive to me through a picture the Lord painted on my imagination. I saw myself bowing down before Him in repentance. As soon as I confessed my sin, He reached down and raised me up to sit beside Jesus at His right hand. As I looked down upon the sin that had enslaved me— the enemy of God—I realized I now have the power to resist and overcome it. I no longer have to be subject to the control of the sin. As I humbled myself before God, He raised me up to gain authority over the very thing holding me captive. I was no longer in the position of an enemy of God. I was now in the favored position of the Son.

Through this prophetic picture, I realize I need to continually embrace repentance in order to remain in and enjoy God's limitless love, grace and power. Through repentance from the sins God reveals, I am freed from the grasp of sin and the deception of God's enemy.

The exercise of repenting of sin and appropriating God's forgiveness keeps you strong and confident in the ever-present love and grace of our Lord. He never tires of a pure and broken heart willing to acknowledge His truth and exercise the power you have to live by it.

As you bow before Him, when you recognize sin in your life, you are actually bringing His enemy to His footstool for judgment. Through your repentance and acknowledgement of His judgment on the sin, He covers you with the blood of Jesus, cleans your heart and raises you up to sit at His right hand and live in victory over the sin. That enemy of your soul is the enemy of His Son. Jesus has given you power to reign over sin and the enemy.

The Lord's footstool is your springboard into righteousness. True repentance moves you forward into God's higher way of life where you can appropriate the power of His love and holiness. Repentance empowers you to live as you see Him living—free from sin and guilt and shame! He reaches down as you repent to bring you out of the destruction sin produces. He reminds you of His authority you have been given over sin. Then, you have the ability to overcome consequences produced by your sin. You can move forward to live an abundant life, produce righteous deeds and reflect His glorious light to others. What a simple but powerful strategy our God has created for us to live vitally and intimately connected to His love and grace!

PRAYER

Father, I pray that you will grant me the gift of repentance for any place in my heart that harbors your enemies. I ask for revelation and understanding of these enemies and freedom from their stronghold in my heart. Thank You for drawing me close and seating me at Your right hand. In Jesus's name, Amen.

Questions for Reflection:

How do you feel about being a resting place for God's presence?

What kind of feelings do you experience when you think of repentance?

What kind of familiar patterns of behavior in your life could keep you bound to an enemy of God?

CHAPTER FOUR

THE REPENTANT KING

We are all subject to the temptations of the flesh and kings are no exception. Today and all throughout history, we have seen many using their high positions of authority and influence for selfish gain. Those in authority have accountability before the Lord to walk in wisdom and a profound responsibility toward those under their leadership. With this privilege of carrying authority comes a weight of responsibility to put the welfare of others before their own personal desires.

And David said to Nathan, I have sinned against the Lord. And Nathan said to David, The Lord also has put away your sin; you shall not die. 2 Samuel 12:13

During David's reign as the king of Israel, he made a self-serving decision that almost cost him his throne and his life. But the account of his mistake sheds great light on the mercy of Father God. His experience exemplifies the process of repentance in a godly life. It is truly a prophetic picture of the grace of God toward a repentant heart. In 2 Samuel 11-12 you can read how David sins as a leader in Israel and seeks repentance from the Lord.

> *It happened in the spring of the year, at the time when kings go out to battle, that David sent Joab and his servants with him, and all Israel, and they destroyed the people of Ammon and besieged Rabbah. But David remained at Jerusalem. 2 Samuel 11:1*

God anointed David to be king of Israel. He hand-picked him out of the sheepfolds, brought him through many trials under the leadership of Saul and put him in the place of reigning. But, on this occasion, David decided not to lead his men into battle as was the custom of kings.

Perhaps David thought he needed some rest and re-laxation—or as abbreviated in the military, R&R. Whatever his reason, he was not walking in the fullness of God as a leader. It is easy to relate to David here. Sometimes the way is long and tiring. Leadership can get wearisome. The yearning for comfort and relief can become strong. But only God can issue R&R for his children.

As David lay in comfort while his army fought, he lusted after Bathsheba and his sin overtook him. His lust motivated him to plan the demise of her husband who was a loyal soldier. That was an outrageous act of selfishness!

As David entertained this evil distraction from responsibility, he backed out of his place of leadership and was deceived into thinking he was above the law of God. No man is above the law of God, including his chosen leaders.

Giving way to the lust of the flesh not only affected David and Bathsheba, but it left a scar on his family and must have caused those who knew him intimately to question his ability to lead Israel into the future. The consequences of his actions reached far beyond his own life.

In spite of this great fall in David's life, God had compassion and pity on him as he repented. In Psalm 51:1-6, David reveals his understanding of the majesty and mercy of his God as well as the depth of his transgression.

> *Have mercy upon me, O God, according to Your lovingkindness; according to the multitude of Your tender mercies, blot out my transgressions. Wash me thoroughly from my iniquity, and cleanse me from my sin. For I acknowledge my transgressions, and my sin is always before me. Against You, You only, have I sinned, and done this evil in Your sight—that You may be found just when You speak, and blameless when You judge. Behold, I was brought forth in iniquity, and in sin my mother conceived me. Behold, You desire truth in the inward parts, and in the hidden part You will make me to know wisdom.*

David leaves no excuses for himself as he surrenders to the judgment of God. He recognizes he is thoroughly unclean. He is painfully distraught and grieved in the depths of his being. He remembers, from the law, he deserves death (Leviticus 20:10 and 24:17). So, David agrees with the Lord.

Whatever sentence He sends will be justified and true. Even under the anointing of king, David was still a man, born of woman and subject to sin. The flesh can never be trusted to lead you to lasting satisfaction. The passing pleasure of sin quickly fades and leaves behind devastation and death. David knew God alone was just and true and he was at the mercy of His righteous judgment.

But how could David have missed the Lord in such a big way? He was more than familiar with the laws of God. He knew right from wrong. I think there is a key in David's own confession that may answer that question.

> *Create in me a clean heart, O God, and renew a steadfast spirit within me. Do not cast me away from Your presence, and do not take Your Holy Spirit from me.*
> *Psalm 51:10-11*

As David continued to behold Bathsheba, day after day, he began to tune out the convicting voice of the Holy Spirit. He ignored what God had spoken to him in the written law and chose to comfort his flesh with her presence instead of the presence of the Lord. David had become so deaf to the voice of the Holy Spirit that God had to send His prophet, Nathan, to speak the truth to David once again. (2 Samuel 12:1)

In verses 12 and 13 of Psalm 51, you can see how David knew God's heart so well. Even in the light of his own sin, he knew to cry out for full restoration from the One and only Redeemer of mankind.

> *Restore to me the joy of Your salvation, and uphold me by Your generous Spirit. Then, I will teach transgressors Your ways, and sinners shall be converted to You.*

Real repentance must bring you to the place of seeing there is no good in you apart from the Spirit of the Living God. You can produce no good in and of yourself. He alone is righteous and true. He alone enables you to be righteous and true.

62

In Psalm 51:6 David cries out for truth in the "inward parts" and wisdom in the "hidden part." Jesus said, **"I am the Way, the Truth and the Life"** (John 14:6). Paul wrote about **"life in Christ Jesus, Whom God made our Wisdom from God"** (1 Corinthians 1:30). Truth and wisdom can only come to you through a vital relationship with Jesus Christ.

Unlike David, through the acceptance of Jesus as Savior of your life, the Spirit of God comes to live within you. He doesn't just rest on you with an anointing. He actually comes to take up residence in your inward parts to bring you His truth and His wisdom.

But how can a born-again believer with the Spirit of God residing in him miss the truth and wisdom of God? The same way David did. You miss God's truth and wisdom by clinging to the truth of your old life and the wisdom of the world. Man's truth and wisdom falls far short of the truth and wisdom of God. The Lord has graciously provided true repentance as our road to restoration and the blood of the Lamb as our escape from eternal separation from Him.

If we say that we have fellowship with Him, and walk in darkness, we lie and do not practice the truth. But if we walk in the light as He is in the light, we have fellowship with one another, and the blood of Jesus Christ His Son cleanses us from all sin. If we say that we have no sin, we deceive ourselves, and the truth is not in us. If we confess our sins, He is faithful and just to forgive us our sins and to cleanse us from all unrighteousness.
1 John 1: 6-9

Realms of Truth

In the dictionary, there are several definitions of truth. I believe three of them form a picture of the realms of truth available to every person. Through the power and revelation of the Holy Spirit, you can move from the lower realms of truth into the highest realm of truth in God.

1. Conformity to fact or reality:

Most of humanity lives in this realm of truth during the majority of life here on earth. You are born into the world relating mainly to the five senses and how you are affected by your surroundings. You respond to whatever enhances and sustains your physical body and natural mind. The natural things around you reveal a basic realm of truth: fire is hot, ice is cold.

2. Conformity to rule, standard, model, pattern or ideal:

You grow intellectually into this next realm of truth. In your formative years, the rules and standards of your family, schools and peers collectively influence your base of truth. From these models your personal ideals and living patterns are formed. You are strongly motivated by them.

The written word of God offers another pattern for truth. The word of God points to your Creator and begins to show you a way of life higher than your natural impulses and learned standards of behavior.

The Law of Moses was the pattern God gave the Israelites as a guideline for higher living. Most of us have tried to change our lives to conform to God's model of truth with our human strength. Like the Israelites, we quickly discover we cannot consistently live in the realm of truth presented in the written Word of God.

3. Conformity to the requirements of one's being or nature:

In this highest realm of truth, you are only able to relate according to the nature resident within you. Natural man is only able to relate to natural things. But the supernatural Father of Life created you to live as His child with His nature.

God intends for you to live consciously aware of Him and His nature abiding within you. Only then are you are able to act according to His righteous truth. The indwelling power of the Holy Spirit enables you to move out of the natural truths of the world. He reveals the supernatural truths of His original purpose for your life. He enables you to walk in the nature of Christ, the Son of God. You are to sound and look like your Father and Lord.

The power of the Holy Spirit restores you to the highest realms of truth that were lost in the Garden of Eden. Adam and Eve gave up God's truth for the lie of the devil. They chose to eat of the tree of good and evil because they believed the words of the enemy of God instead of the Living Word of God. The resurrection power of Jesus secured for you the ability to choose between the low truth of the enemy of God and the highest truth of your Creator (See Genesis 3).

Father God desires for you to live above the struggle of simply conforming to a standard. He comes to completely replace your worldly nature with His holy nature so you can live in the redeeming Truth of God. As you seek His presence, He patiently draws you upward from the realms of natural truths ushering you into the realm of His redemptive super-natural truth.

True Reality

God created dogs to behave like dogs and cats to behave like cats. They are both animals, but have distinct natural characteristics making them different in behavior. They have no choice but to behave like a dog or a cat.

But God created man and woman in His own image with the ability to think and act and choose. He designed you with the ability to have intimate relationship with Him as a child. So, God's intent for you is to respond to life on earth out of the divine nature He originally created within you. Unlike animals, you have the power to choose what truth you will live by—divine or natural.

As you continue to agree with God and obey His Word and His Spirit, He reveals to you the divine truth of your real identity. He cleans and purifies every part of your life so you can begin to live like the person He created you to be.

Bill Johnson stated in his book *Dreaming with God,* "The sanctified imagination is a tool in God's hand that enables us to tap into true reality." Worship and repentance at the footstool of God transforms your imagination. You are enabled by His presence to receive the highest truth of your identity as a child of God, created in the image of Christ Jesus. The Holy Spirit is then able to impart revelations to you from the heart of the Father that can change you and your world.

On the day of Pentecost, Peter addresses the people quoting one of David's psalms:

> *You have made known to me the ways of life; You will enrapture me [diffusing my soul with joy] with and in Your presence. Psalm 16:11 (Amplified Bible)*

Peter and David both knew that God's presence opened up the reality of His kingdom truth and brought joy and purpose to every life. God's desire is for each of us to live in this kingdom reality free from the bondage of sin, living out our divine destiny on earth.

Learning to see ourselves the way God sees us.

A Cry for Purity

In Psalm 51:6 David cried out **"to know wisdom in his inmost heart."** You need the Holy Spirit to show you how to assimilate and apply His truth for the highest purposes of God. Jesus asked the Father to send the Holy Spirit as His representative of the truth and wisdom of God (John 14:15). The Holy Spirit teaches and imparts your true nature within you.

In Psalm 51:7 David calls for God to purge him with hyssop. The word "purge" means purify[1]. Hyssop was a plant used in sprinkling the blood of sacrifices and in ceremonial cleansing of lepers. It was also used to give sour wine to Jesus as he hung on the cross just before He died. You also need the purifying hyssop of God's truth to purge your inmost heart before real death to self comes and resurrection life can be imparted.

The Lord spoke to the prophet Jeremiah saying:

The heart is deceitful above all things, and desperately wicked: who can know it? I, the Lord, search the heart, I try the reins, even to give every man according to his ways, according to the fruit of his doings. Jeremiah 17:9-10

The word **heart** figuratively means the feelings, will and even the intellect.[2] The Lord says *He* will "search the heart." *God alone can do this work of searching the heart.* He alone can shine the light on deceptive thinking and corrupt motives.

He also wants to "try the reins." This figuratively means the mind (as the interior self)[3]. The interior self repre-

69

sents the seat of the affections and passions of your soul. The Lord will test or purge your affections and motives with the heat of His desire just as you would test the purity of metal with fire. God is looking for the precious metal of Jesus in your inner man. He will lovingly purge out the pollution (the lower truths) in the soul. He cleanses it with His blood. Then, He tenderly replaces it all with the pure gold of His truth.

Stand therefore [hold your ground], having tightened the belt of truth around your loins... Ephesians 6:14a

The **loins** represent the procreative power of man. Your ability to reproduce the character of Jesus through your life is vulnerable to attack from the enemy of your soul. Without this purging of the heart, you are left without a vital piece of your spiritual armor. You cannot reproduce the likeness of Jesus Christ in the earth without His higher truth surrounding and protecting your inner man.

God's truth in your inner man builds a stronghold around your heart that protects against the craftiness and temptations of the enemy of your soul. The truth of God's word also creates within your heart a pure place in which the Father, Son and Holy Spirit can come to rest and fellowship with you continually.

His Resting Place

Jesus, the Living Word, finds a resting place within your heart as you allow Him to compassionately purge your soul. The Holy Spirit will bring the revelation of the Father's righteousness and gracious favor into your life. Then, the Creator and Lover of your soul will take His rightful place on the throne of your heart. His loving, powerful presence will transform you as you embrace the footstool of His rest. David cried out for God's truth:

> *Teach me Your way, O Lord, that I may walk and live in Your truth; direct and **unite my heart** (solely, reverently) to fear and honor Your name. I will confess and praise You, O Lord my God, with my whole (united) heart; and I will glorify Your name forevermore. Psalm 86:11-12 (Amplified Bible)*

The path of repentance and cleansing brings wholeness to your divided heart. Your spirit, soul and body were created to be unified and whole like Father, Son and Holy Spirit. God is triune in nature and so are you. God's truth unites your life and enables you to reflect His divine wholeness. You can live in true harmony as you follow His truth.

All this work of purging and cleansing can appear daunting at first. But the Lord is so gentle and patient in bringing the gift of repentance. When the first taste of freedom and victory over an enemy of your soul comes, it produces a hunger and thirst for more liberty. The road to freedom is often difficult. But the sweetness of victory will propel you into the next battle with great expectation for the abundant goodness of God.

Recently, I received a simple revelation about the convicting light of God as I was walking through my kitchen. It was a clear day and the morning sun was shining brightly into the window over my sink. The bright light was like a spotlight on a dark stage. I had just cleaned the countertops and washed the morning dishes. On the surface everything looked neat and clean.

As I followed the stream of light coming in the window, it landed on the side of the kitchen island cabinet in the center of the room. It is painted black and the overhead lights do not shine on the sides of that cabinet. The sunshine revealed a disgusting deposit of spilled, dried foods and a thick layer of dust that I had completely overlooked. In the busyness of life, I had obviously overlooked the cleaning of the island cabinet because I could not easily see the buildup of grime. Ugh!

As I quickly went to work scrubbing away the mess, the Lord reminded me that only His Son's light would reveal those dark inner places of my heart that needed cleansing. The warmth of that morning sun in my kitchen was so inviting, but it was also very revealing. I think that is the way the Lord deals with us as we continue to behold His glory and listen to His voice. He gently, but thoroughly, unveils the hidden enemies in our hearts so we can be free to shine with His pure goodness.

From Repentance to Restoration

Remember that David's whole life, even his frailties and failures, became a prophetic picture of the redeeming power of the love of God that would come through the blood of Christ Jesus. God displayed His glorious restoration through this simple shepherd boy who became the king of Israel and the ancestor of Jesus, our Lord.

Below is David's entire prayer of repentance as written by Brian Simmons in his Passion Translation of Psalm 51. As you read, take careful notice of how David moves from deep sorrow into triumphant hope for himself and his nation in the presence of his God.

God give me grace from your fountain of forgiveness! I know your abundant love is enough to wash away my guilt. Take away this shameful guilt of sin. Forgive the full extent of my wrong and erase this deep stain on my conscience for I am ashamed. I feel such pain and anguish within me, I can't get away from the sting of my sin against you, Lord! Everything I did, I did right in front of you, for you saw it all. Everything you say to me is infallibly true and your judgment conquers me. Lord, I have been a sinner from birth. Sin's corruption has polluted my soul. I know that you delight to set your truth deep in my spirit. So come into the hidden places of my heart and teach me wisdom. Purify my conscience! Make this leper clean again! Wash me in your love until I am pure in heart. Satisfy me in your sweetness, and my song of joy will return. The places within me you have crushed will rejoice in your healing touch. Hide my sins from your face; erase all my guilt in your saving grace. Start over with me, and create a new, clean heart with me. Fill me with pure thoughts and holy desires, ready to please you. May there never be even

*a shadow of darkness between us! May you never de-
prive me of your Sacred Spirit! Let my passion for life
be restored, tasting joy in every breakthrough you
bring to me. Give me more of your Holy Spirit-Wind, so
that I may stand strong and true to you! Then I can
show to other guilty ones how loving and merciful you
are. They will find their way back home to you, knowing that you will forgive them. O God, my saving God,
deliver me fully from every sin, even the sin that
brought blood-guilt to my soul. Then my heart will once
again be thrilled to sing the passionate songs of righteousness and forgiveness! Lord God, unlock my heart,
unlock my lips, and I will overcome with my joyous
praise! For the source of your pleasure is not in my
performance or the sacrifices I might offer to you. The
fountain of your pleasure is found in the sacrifice of my
shattered heart before you. You will not despise my
tenderness as I humbly bow down at your feet! Lord,
don't punish others for my sin; keep showing favor to
Zion. Be the protecting wall around Jerusalem. And
when we are fully restored you will rejoice and take delight in every offering of our lives; as we bring our
every sacrifice of righteousness before you in love!*

Even though David knew that the laws of the Lord
called for his death because of his sin, he somehow knew in
his heart that his God was filled with mercy and would restore
him and the country to righteousness and wholeness again. He
trusted the Lord to use his own failures as an example to others, showing the compassion and goodness of God toward
hearts filled with true repentance.

David was a man who lived under the Old Covenant
with God, but carried the New Covenant of God within his
heart. His whole life pointed to the One who would pay the

ultimate price for the sin of mankind and restore them to their loving and forgiving Creator.

As the Lord leads you down the road of worship and repentance, you will be transformed into the likeness of Christ Jesus. You will progressively become equipped to take ground for the Kingdom of God on the earth. He will mold you into a mighty person who can carry the authority of your King.

Father God is longing to make you into a resting place for His glory and power. As you meditate on His generous and powerful grace and goodness, He will supply you with abundant courage to look at any strongholds that His enemies may have built in your heart. You can live life fully enjoying His presence and power and restoration. You can become like David—a man (or woman) after God's own heart!

PRAYER

Father, I desire to follow Jesus into the fullness of the life You created for me. Thank You for loving me enough to send Your most precious Son to lead me into a righteous lifestyle that will glorify You and equip me to fulfill the destiny You have planned for me. By Your grace and mercy and the power of Holy Spirit, I choose to walk with You in humility and authority. In Jesus's mighty name, Amen.

Questions for Reflection:

How does taking on leadership responsibility make you feel?

What are you afraid of as you think of being responsible for carrying the presence of God?

How do you think God would like to help you be a godly influence in the earth?

PSALM 110:2

The Lord will send forth from Zion
the scepter of Your strength;
rule then, in the midst of Your foes.

The Message - You were forged a
strong scepter by God of Zion,
now rule, though surrounded
by enemies!

CHAPTER FIVE

WHERE TO WE GO FROM HERE?

It is hard for most of us to imagine what it would be like to carry the power and authority of a king. We have little understanding of the responsibility or the privilege that a sovereign ruler would exercise. Nor do we fully understand the pressures of opposing forces that a ruler might encounter as he tries to execute his authority within his kingdom.

The Lord has called His people to rule and reign with Him. He desires to create in you a place for His power to dwell and His love to flourish. He created you to be actively involved in the work of building the Kingdom of God in the earth. This idea of reigning with God sparks the imagination and produces a great weight of responsibility. How do you live in this position throughout your daily life?

A close look at the second verse of this amazing psalm unlocks some clues. In this verse David prophetically describes how Jehovah will enable the Lord to rule in the midst of His foes. David experienced the ruling power of God throughout his life, including the times when he was surrounded by his enemies.

Jehovah called David to be king of Israel long before he actually took the position of authority on a throne. He was only a youth when Samuel anointed him to become God's choice for king. It took many years of isolation, opposition and warfare to equip David to actually assume his place on the throne of Israel. David's patient and persistent obedience to the word of the Lord positioned him to be chosen as king by the Israelites. But David ruled with the authority of God long before he was recognized as a ruler by men.

Soon after the death of King Saul and his son, all the elders of Israel came to David and made a covenant with him to assume the position of king. At the age of thirty, David began his forty-year reign. Very soon after becoming king, he led his army into battle against the Jebusites, cunningly captured the stronghold of Zion and declared it to be the City of David (2 Samuel 5).

Zion became the physical site for the seat of God's authority over Israel. God equipped David to be His scepter of authority reaching into his nation and beyond. David consistently led his armies out to conquer Israel's enemies. From this geographical location, with the power and abundance of God, David enlarged the territory of Israel and set up the government of God over His chosen nation. Zion, which was once the stronghold of the enemies of God, became the earthly dwelling place for His peace and power.

Building a Resting Place for God

Psalm 132 records the deep desire in David to build a permanent resting place for the presence of God. David was desperate to bring the Ark of the Testimony (Exodus 25:10-22) into Zion. He wanted to build a home for this symbol of God's presence within Israel. Everywhere the Ark rested it brought prosperity, abundance and protection. David believed the Ark must remain in their midst to insure the continued success and prosperity of the nation.

As David pours out his desire before the Lord, God promises to abide with Israel and bless her for generations to come:

> *The Lord has sworn in truth to David; He will not turn from it: "I will set upon your throne the fruit of your body,*
>
> *If your sons will keep My covenant and My testimony which I shall teach them, their sons also shall sit upon your throne forevermore."*
>
> *For the Lord has chosen Zion; He has desired it for His dwelling place:*
>
> *"This is My resting place forever; here will I dwell, for I have desired it.*
>
> *I will abundantly bless her provision; I will satisfy her poor with bread.*
>
> *I will also clothe her priests with salvation, and her saints shall shout aloud for joy. There I will make the horn of David grow; I will prepare a lamp for My Anointed. His enemies I will clothe with shame, but upon Himself His crown shall flourish." Psalm 132:11-18*

This was God's covenant promise to David and his children. It is also a prophetic picture of God's anointed Son as He takes His seat of authority after the cross and the resurrection. Jesus is a direct descendant of David and He reigns from on high, seated on the Throne of God in the heavenly Zion.

For David, Zion was an earthly representation of God's seat of authority. For Christians, Zion symbolizes God's authority within the Body of Christ. Every believer who bows at the feet of God's Son, recognizing His authority to rule their lives can become a scepter in the hand of God, just like David. If you are a Christian, you are called to be a carrier of God's power, reflecting His glory into your territory in the earth.

The King's Scepter

During David's time in history, it was common for rulers to carry a scepter as a symbol of the power and authority of their office. If anyone approached the throne, the scepter would be extended in favor or sometimes in hostility as they came near. The scepter was used to bless or curse those who dared to enter the presence of the ruling authority.

In the Old Testament, the rod or scepter was used as a symbol of the power and authority God granted to those He called to be leaders. The following scriptures are examples:

Exodus 4:20-21: God turned Moses' rod into an instrument to perform signs and wonders in the courts of Pharaoh. Eventually, because of these displays of power, Pharaoh released the Israelites from bondage.

Numbers 17:8-10: All the heads of the tribes of Israel carried rods. Only Aaron's rod bloomed as a sign of God's favor on Moses and Aaron and their power to rule. The blooming rod was a sign to the rebellious people who murmured and complained about their appointed leaders.

Ezekiel 19:10-14: The prophet speaks of the ruling rods of Israel being cast down and consumed in God's wrath because of their unrighteousness. Their strength and power to rule ceased because of their sin. Only people with a holy reverence for God's authority in their lives are able to stand in the midst of opposition and maintain the inherited power and strength given to them by God. The strength of a man or a nation can only continue as they submit to God's rule in their midst. Otherwise, they become captives and slaves to ungodliness and eventually face God's judgment.

Micah 6:1-9: The Lord called Jerusalem to account to plead their case before Him. Heeding God's chosen servant (rod) as the voice of His authority was to be an act of bowing at the footstool of God. The prophet Micah was God's chosen mouthpiece. He was given authority to proclaim God's word to the city of Jerusalem. Rebellion against godly authorities is not an option for those who would call themselves by His name.

In these examples, it is apparent that God sends forth His power and authority through ordinary people who live in His presence and heed His word. They become rods or extensions of His presence because of their intimacy with Him.

In the original Hebrew language, **scepter** means a rod or, literally, a branch.[1] This meaning gives us a better picture of the Lord extending his ruling strength like a branch is extended from a tree. The branch is attached to the trunk and only has life and strength as it remains one with the tree. Jesus explained the idea of being an extension of God.

I am the Vine; you are the branches. Whoever lives in Me and I in him bears much (abundant) fruit. However, apart from Me [cut off from vital union with Me] you can do nothing.

If a person does not dwell in Me, he is thrown out like a [broken-off] branch, and withers; such branches are gathered up and thrown into the fire, and they are burned.

If you live in Me [abide vitally united to Me] and My words remain in you and continue to live in your hearts, ask whatever you will, and it shall be done for you.

When you bear (produce) much fruit, My Father is honored and glorified, and you show and prove your-selves to be true followers of Mine. John 15:6-8 (Amplified Bible).

The Lord's power and authority resides in you when you bow at the feet of Jesus in repentance and adoration. You are raised up to sit by Him at the right hand of the Father. As you walk in obedience to the plans and purposes of God for your own life, you carry His strength and wisdom for ruling into the places of responsibility and influence He gives you.

Ruling in the Midst of Your Foes

In this second verse of Psalm 110, the Father promises Jesus He will extend His victorious strength through Zion (the Church). Therefore, the authority of Jesus Himself enables those who have surrendered to the Lordship of Jesus to rule in the center of His enemies. You can become a rod in His hand sent forth from your place of intimacy with Jesus. When you acknowledge His Living Word, He is able to rule in the center of your being where His enemies once ruled.

I believe there is another way to look at this verse. Before David became king, he served under the rule of Saul whom God had raised up to be the king of the Israelites. Saul progressively became self-focused. He was literally mentally disturbed. He ruled according to the mandates of his flesh instead of the word of the Lord in that day.

During the time that David served as a leader in Saul's army, he became increasingly more popular with the people. Saul became intensely jealous of him, and David had to flee for his life. He hid in caves to avoid Saul's wrath. He was forced to band together with thieves and exiles in order to stay alive.

Even during this time of darkness and despair, David proved his ability to rule. He built his band of misfits into a well-defined army. They respected him and followed him loyally. Even when he had the opportunity to kill Saul, David remembered God alone had allowed Saul to be king. He waited on God to do what He desired with Saul.

Then the men of David said to him, "This is the day of which the Lord said to you, 'Behold, I will deliver your enemy into your hand that you may do to him as it seems good to you.'" And David arose and secretly cut off a corner of Saul's robe. Now it happened afterward that David's heart troubled him because he had cut Saul's robe. And he said to his men, "The Lord forbid that I should do this thing to my master, the Lord's anointed, to stretch out my hand against him, seeing he is the anointed of the Lord." So David restrained his servants with these words, and did not allow them to rise against Saul. 1 Samuel 24:4-7

David honored Saul as the reigning authority of Israel. He trusted the Lord to do with Saul as He desired. In the place of hiding, David decided to rule in the midst of his enemy's presence. He chose to use his God-promised authority to honor Saul even though he had become a rebellious king. David trusted His Lord to bring him into authority in God's own timing and in His own way.

While Jesus walked on the earth, He knew He was the Son of God, but He obediently chose the way of the cross, which led Him into the center of His enemy's domain. He could have relied on force and the power of the sword to bring about an earthly dominion. Instead, He chose obedience to death to face the real enemy of His kingdom, the enemy of men's souls.

Therefore He says: "When He ascended on high, He led captivity captive, and gave gifts to men." (Now this, "He ascended"—what does it mean but that He also first descended into the lower parts of the earth? He who descended is also the One who ascended far above

all the heavens, that He might fill all things.) Ephesians
4:8-10 (Amplified Bible)

Jesus ruled in the midst of His earthly enemies. He did not allow them to cut off the amazing plan of His Father. He defeated the devil in his own domain, opening the prison doors that held His creation in darkness and deception. In the face of what looked like total defeat to His followers, Jesus was continuing to rule as He suffered. He died so He could gain access to enemy territory and win an eternal victory!

Today, the Body of Christ has the ability to rule and reign with the same resurrection power of Jesus. You can defeat the enemy of your soul. You can lead many others out of darkness into the eternal light of His presence. You can become a powerful rod of God's strength as you bow before Him in worship and obedience. By His grace, you can lay down your comfort, convenience, privileges and even your very life. You can open up avenues of healing, deliverance and blessing for those who are still enemies of the living King of Heaven!

The Dream Continues

David perceived a geographical place with a physical building as the resting place of His God. His desire went so deep that God favored David with the ways and means to prepare for the construction of his dream. David did not build the glorious temple he had envisioned. However, God enabled him to pass the dream and the plan on to Solomon, his son.

Thus, the next generation was brought into the plans and purposes of God without interruption. The dream to produce an example of the everlasting glory of God was passed from father to son. It was an earthly reflection of the Father's delight in giving His Son. Jesus is the power and provision to bring creation back into intimate fellowship with the Godhead.

Jesus is the scepter of the Father's authority. He came into this fallen world to wield righteous authority over His enemies and open the door of salvation to man. The Lord is calling the Church to maturity, unity, humility and pure worship before the Throne of God. His desire is for the Church to reign with Him in love and authority.

As a believer who worships and repents at the footstool of Jesus, you will be raised up and sent forth as a scepter, extending the favor and the fury of God into your realm of influence. You will overcome God's enemies through His wisdom and become a willing carrier of God's presence, passion and authority. You will influence others to follow you to the footstool of His presence and learn to rule with Him in the midst of all His enemies.

If then you were raised with Christ, seek those things which are above, where Christ is, sitting at the right hand of God. Set your mind on things above, not on things on the earth. For you died, and your life is hidden with Christ in God. When Christ who is our life appears, then you also will appear with Him in glory. Colossians 3:1-4

It is time for all who call themselves Christians to take courage and come boldly before your compassionate God, who sits upon the throne of grace, and surrender your right to rule your own lives. It is time to honor His heart's desire to make you scepters in His hand to extend His presence and power into the places you live. It is time to become passionate volunteers.

PRAYER

Father, I hear You calling me into the responsibility of reigning and ruling as a scepter in Your hand. I thank You for the courage and grace to follow You into my destiny as your child, to carry your authority with love and wisdom to a lost and dying world. Open my eyes and ears to receive your instructions and change the desires of my heart to match the desires of Your heart. In Jesus's name, Amen

Questions for Reflection:

What does godly authority look like to you?

true
humility

Jesus
no fear of man
obedience to the Word

How do you feel about being responsible to lead others into a relationship with the Lord?

How is the Lord leading you to take on more responsibility to draw others into His presence?

91

PSALM 110:3

Your people shall be volunteers in the day of Your power;
in the beauties of holiness, from the womb of the morning,
You have the dew of Your youth.

(Jesus')
"Your people will freely join
You, resplendent in holy armor
on the great day of Your conquest,
join You at the fresh break of
day, join You with all the
vigor of youth" (The Message)

93

CHAPTER SIX

PASSION PRODUCES NEW LIFE

Have you ever volunteered to do something and later wondered why you got involved? I think that is a common experience for most of us. Often our perception of an activity is not realistic. We like the idea of helping someone or accomplishing some task that sparks our interest, but we have little understanding of the costs involved in carrying it out completely. It sounded exciting, stimulating and maybe even a bit romantic and dreamy. We have all been there and done that for sure. Even so, volunteering is a great way to learn and grow.

True volunteers are passionate people. Their passion guides their performance and perpetuates their energy. Their actions are fueled by deep, heart-felt emotions. They are eager to invest whatever time and talents they have to pursue their passion.

The word "volunteers," in this third verse of Psalm 110, comes from a Hebrew word which means *spontaneous.*

In Webster's dictionary, the word spontaneous has these meanings:

1. Arising without external constraint or stimulus;
2. Arising from a momentary impulse;
3. Controlled and directed internally;
4. Produced without being planted or without human labor;
5. Developing without apparent external force, cause or treatment;
6. Not apparently contrived or manipulated: *natural.*[1]

Spontaneous, voluntary actions come from the heart. Volunteers come forward at a moment's notice to act and speak as the opportunity arises. Their actions can look impulsive at times because their enthusiasm pushes them. They are not overly concerned with unexpected difficulties they might encounter. They just want to be actively involved with the passion of their soul.

Jesus is the perfect example of a volunteer. The Father did not force Him to leave the glory of Heaven—He volunteered. The Father did not coerce Him to die for your sins—He volunteered. He was not pushed into hell to confront the powers of the enemy—He volunteered. Jesus chose to give Himself completely for people who did not know or care about Him. He volunteered because of His selfless love for the Father and His passion for creation.

Today, is the Church operating with a spontaneous heart of devotion to Christ or to their self-serving agendas? Has true devotion to Christ been superseded by the desire to have personal needs met? Is spontaneity being replaced by organizational strategies and planned programs?

As you become a resting place for the presence of God, a dwelling for His virtue and character, you will spontaneously respond to His calls for action. While organization and planning can be helpful in executing a call of the Lord, the impact of a passionate volunteer will surpass the methodology of a passionless professional every time.

In Psalm 110:3 David describes a people with this same voluntary passion who will follow the Lord. From the very beginning of Jesus' ministry on earth, He ignited passion in the souls of men and women everywhere He went.

Spontaneous Disciples

A relationship with Jesus was a continuous exercise in spontaneity for His disciples. He was constantly presenting them with opportunities to be spontaneous. His first personal encounter with three of His disciples was that kind of opportunity.

Peter, James and John had been fishing all night and were on the shore of the Sea of Galilee cleaning their nets. Jesus decided to climb into Peter's boat to address the crowd that had gathered to hear Him speak. Spontaneously, He asked Peter to pull the boat slightly offshore. Peter had previously witnessed the healing powers of Jesus when He healed his mother-in-law of a serious fever. Probably out of respect for Jesus, Peter complied with the request and moved the boat so Jesus could speak to the crowd.

After Jesus spoke to the people, He made another request of Peter. He asked him to move out into the deeper water and lower his fishing nets again. Peter had no logical reason for obeying this untimely request from Jesus. After all, Peter was an experienced fisherman and had just spent all night casting his net with nothing to show for all his hard work. He seemed convinced that the effort would be fruitless.

Peter responded with a respectful but doubtful heart,

"Master, we toiled all night and caught nothing; nevertheless at Your word I will let down the net." Luke 5:5

Peter's respect for Jesus prompted and energized him to perform the task even though his own mind reasoned it would be to no avail. Peter's heart, not his expertise as a fisherman, guided his actions.

The result of this spontaneous encounter with Jesus proved to be amazing to the weary fisherman. Peter's nets became so full he needed help from James and John to pull them up. The catch was so abundant that all their boats began to sink from the weight of the fish.

At this point, Peter could have been consumed with the abundance of his catch and focused on the wealth of provision he had before him. He could have stayed with the catch, fed all their families, made a lot of money and expanded his business with the profits. Instead, Peter spontaneously responded to Jesus with repentance and worship.

When Simon Peter saw it, he fell down at Jesus' knees, saying, "Depart from me, for I am a sinful man, O Lord!" For he and all who were with him were astonished at the catch of fish which they had taken; and so also were James and John, the sons of Zebedee, who were partners with Simon. Luke 5:8-10

Peter's response to Jesus' spontaneous request became an opportunity for change. The encounter not only changed Peter's heart, but also the hearts of his partners. It was just the beginning of a relationship that would change the course of their lives and the course of history! As Peter bowed at the feet of Jesus in repentance, he was changed from a toiling fisherman into a willing fisher of men.

And Jesus said to Simon, "Do not be afraid. From now on you will catch men." So when they had brought their

Although Peter had seen the healing power of Jesus, he did not fully devote himself to Him. Jesus met the mother-in-law at her point of need, but He met Peter at his workplace, where he devoted most of his time and energies. The encounter became an intimate exchange between Peter and Jesus. Jesus knew Peter and what would speak to him most effectively.

Jesus meets you in the places that deeply impact your individual life. If you obediently respond to His call for action, He will meet you with personal and powerful encounters creating voluntary responses of abandoned worship. Obedience should lead to greater intimacy and devotion.

If you keep My commandments [if you continue to obey My instructions], you will abide in My love and live on in it, just as I have obeyed My Father's commandments and live on in His love. I have told you these things, that My joy and delight may be in you, and that your joy and gladness may be of full measure and complete and overflowing. John 15:10-11 (Amplified Bible)

The Lord will always present you with opportunities that require more than you are able to give. As you move past your inadequacy and trust in His word, He provides what you lack and reveals His greatness to you in new ways. His calls for action are unique invitations to discover more of His character, love and joy.

Another Spontaneous Worshipper

One of the hallmarks of a sincere volunteer is their lack of self-consciousness and the intense focus on their heart's devotion. An excellent example of this kind of voluntary action is recorded in Luke 7. Jesus was invited to a Pharisee's house to dine and mingle with his friends. When Jesus entered his home, the Pharisee did not even show him the common courtesy of having his servants wash Jesus's feet.

However, a sinfully wicked woman of the town somehow made her way into the Pharisee's home and began to weep at the feet of Jesus and wash them with her tears. Then, she wiped His feet with her hair and began to kiss them tenderly and anointed them with costly perfume. This bold woman seems to have followed Jesus very closely. She had been touched by His words and actions and she had a strong response building within her heart.

Obviously, she had a sordid reputation within her community. She was probably a prostitute and maybe a liar and thief by reputation. The Pharisee, and most likely his guests, had strong judgments formed concerning her value and worth as a person.

But the opinions of those she dwelt among in the community did not seem to deter her passionate expressions of devotion to Jesus. She used all she had at her disposal to express her feelings toward Him. Washing His feet was a sign of respect and honor; anointing His feet with perfume was an act of blessing and generosity; her kisses expressed her pure affection for the man, Christ Jesus.

To the Pharisee, these expressions appeared to be an outrageously lewd demonstration of her bad character. She was using the very tools of her trade as a prostitute to display herself to a man considered, by some, as a teacher and a prophet. Jesus's reaction to these spontaneous expressions of devotion is astounding. He skillfully displays His anointing as Teacher and Prophet by presenting a riddle to the Pharisee.

> *"There was a certain creditor who had two debtors. One owed five hundred denarii, and the other fifty. And when they had nothing with which to repay, he freely forgave them both. Tell Me, therefore, which of them will love him more?"*
>
> *Simon answered and said, "I suppose the one whom he forgave more." Luke 7:41-43a*

When the Pharisee answers the riddle correctly, he receives a rebuke from the Lord and the woman is forgiven of her sins and praised for her faith.

> *"Therefore I say to you, her sins, which are many, are forgiven, for she loved much. But to whom little is forgiven, the same loves little." Then He said to her, "Your sins are forgiven...Your faith has saved you. Go in peace." Luke 7:47-50*

With amazing wisdom, Jesus uncovered the true motives of both the woman and the Pharisee. When the Pharisee failed to honor Jesus with common hospitality, his true heart toward Jesus was exposed. But the woman's true devotion was clearly seen by her willingness to pour out her heart toward Jesus. She risked being exposed to ridicule and cruel rejection in order to humble herself before the One she loved.

Jesus exalted the sinner from the lowest place at His feet to a place of salvation and freedom. He exposed the religious Pharisee's pride and arrogance. The woman was set free and the Pharisee's heart was revealed. Relationship with Jesus produces freedom and life, while religion produces pride and death.

In *My Utmost for His Highest*, Oswald Chambers makes this staggering comment: "We actually slander and dishonor God by our very eagerness to serve Him without knowing Him."[2] Although the Pharisee knew the scriptures, he did not recognize the long-promised Messiah of the scriptures. But this sinful, uneducated woman had discovered Jesus was her God and her Savior and sought to serve Him with her surrender.

You were created to be a spontaneous, voluntary lover of the Lord of Life. He longs for you to be a passionate person who will lay down your own comfort and reputation to experience His life-giving presence.

The Day of Power

David knew this vision of the voluntary people of God would be made manifest in the *day of His power*. The word "day" in this phrase, when translated from the Hebrew, can mean the warm hours of a 24-hour period or it can mean an age or season.[3] I believe David perceived a future age when the Lord's power would produce passionate, worshiping volunteers.

We are living in that age of the Lord's power. Through the birth, life, death and resurrection of His Son, the Father God has moved all who accept Him as Savior out of the age of darkness into the age of light. A new day has dawned.

> *...giving thanks to the Father who has qualified us to be partakers of the inheritance of the saints in the light. He has delivered us from the power of darkness and conveyed us into the kingdom of the Son of His love, in whom we have redemption through His blood, the forgiveness of sins. Colossians1:12-14*

The veil of darkness was taken away in Christ. By beholding the glory of the risen Savior, the Living Word of God, you are transformed out of darkness into His wonderful light of love. In this new day of His resurrection power, you can get an intimate view of His beautiful countenance and enjoy face-to-face encounters as Moses did.

> *Therefore, since we have such hope, we use great boldness of speech—unlike Moses, who put a veil over his face so that the children of Israel could not look steadily at the end of what was passing away. But their minds*

were blinded. For until this day the same veil remains unlifted in the reading of the Old Testament, because the veil is taken away in Christ. But even to this day, when Moses is read, a veil lies on their heart. Nevertheless when one turns to the Lord, the veil is taken away. Now the Lord is the Spirit; and where the Spirit of the Lord is, there is liberty. But we all, with unveiled face, beholding as in a mirror the glory of the Lord, are being transformed into the same image from glory to glory, just as by the Spirit of the Lord. 2 Corinthians 3:12-18

Moses's glorious encounters with the Lord set him apart from the rest of the Israelites. His very countenance was changed each time he came into the presence of the Lord. The face of Moses literally reflected God's holiness. Through Christ, you can also carry the beauty of holiness and the power of transformation.

The Hebrew word for "power" literally means force, whether of men, means or other resources; an army, wealth, virtue, valor, strength.[4] It is derived from the Hebrew root word meaning to twist or whirl, i.e. to dance, to wait, to bring forth, hope, look, be grieved, rest, tarry, travail, tremble, trust, wait carefully, be wounded.[5] The power of the risen Savior is raising up an army of virtuous, valiant, strong men and women. They will work with Him and the resources He provides to bring forth the Kingdom of God on the earth. They will participate in the activities that take place in the presence of God's power.

As a worshipper of His greatness, you will become silenced in awe, find rest for your weary soul and learn to trust and hope in Him. You will be wounded by conviction, experience sorrow and grief for your sin and the sins of others. You will learn to dance and rejoice in His goodness. You will travail and bring forth new life in the spirit through intercession. You will tremble at His Word and learn to watch and wait carefully.

These activities characterize the lives of all God's volunteers. They emerge from the womb of intimate communion with the Living God as a beautiful, holy people reflecting the glory of their risen King and Lord.

The Power of Worship

As a voluntary worshipper, you carry a power that supersedes the power of God's archenemy, the devil. If you remember, Satan was an angel of high degree. He was one created with great beauty and ability to worship the Creator. But his beauty and ability did not keep him from envying the power and attention that the Lord Himself held. He was jealous for the worship given to God. As a result he was cast from heaven with the angels that followed his deception and became the enemy of his own Creator.

In Matthew 4, you can see the account of Satan's attempt to convince Jesus to worship him. Of course, the Lord refused and passed this test in the desert before He began His earthly ministry. As a man, Jesus had to endure this temptation to worship the enemy who desires to be elevated to the place of authority that God alone should hold over mankind. Satan holds no authority in the life of one who totally and wholeheartedly worships the Lord.

And whatever you do [no matter what it is] in word or deed, do everything in the name of the Lord Jesus and in [dependence upon] His Person, giving praise to God the Father through Him. Colossians 3:17 (Amplified Bible)

Every aspect of your life should be worship unto God. Worship is not just a song and a prayer. Worship is a lifestyle. As you submit to His Word and the leading of the Holy Spirit, you are worshiping the Lord because you are showing Him your reverence by living according to His desires. Your relationships, your jobs, your rest and recreation can all become worship as you devote it to Him through obedience and joy.

Satan abandoned the worship of God and became God's enemy. You are called to embrace God in worship and defeat God's enemy!

The Womb of the Morning

There is nothing more exquisite than a beautiful sunrise. When the sun breaks over the horizon, it pierces the darkness and magically lights up the sky with brilliant shafts of color. The whole earth seems to come alive. The birds begin to sing, shapes and forms begin to emerge from the darkness and the activity of life starts afresh with new energy.

Just as the darkness of night covers the life of creation, sin covers the life God created you to live. When the light of Christ dawns on you, you are literally born again into the family of the Trinity: Father, Son and Holy Spirit. You become like a little child, wide-eyed and full of curiosity and enthusiasm. As you are set free from the activities of God's enemies in your soul and live boldly as His child, you come alive with new vision, new passion and fresh energy.

God does not mean for this wonderful phenomenon to end with your salvation prayer. Every time you bow before the Lord in worship and prayer, your youth can be renewed. These times with the Lord are like the nurturing atmosphere of a womb. You are nourished, protected and healed. You grow into a person who can live and move and have their being out in the world without being destroyed. You come away with new hope, new insight and new strength, and His glory shines through you.

You don't have to live in the darkness anymore. Every day becomes a day of power as you offer yourself to Him in intimate fellowship. You experience the glory of the Lord in your own life by beholding Christ, the Living Word. Each new morning brings an opportunity to tap into God's agenda for the day ahead. In His presence, you can behold Him in the written Word of God, in praise and worship, repentance and prayers of petition. You can gain insight, encouragement, strength and freedom to move forward in the destiny He has planned for you.

At any hour of the day, you can enter a realm of relationship and intercession that will bring forth His purposes and plans, not only for yourself, but for your family, church, city and nation. Intimate time with the Lord changes you from being a churchgoer into a Kingdom builder. His power is available to you daily as you volunteer to be His scepter in the earth.

Before Jesus went to the cross, He prayed a prayer of sanctification over His disciples and all those who would ever believe in His name. This priestly prayer set the stage for the dawn of the age of grace and the birth of the Church, the Body of Christ on earth.

But now I come to You, and these things I speak in the world, that they may have My joy fulfilled in themselves. I have given them Your word; and the world has hated them because they are not of the world, just as I am not of the world. I do not pray that You should take them out of the world, but that You should keep them from the evil one. They are not of the world, just as I am not of the world. Sanctify them by Your truth. Your word is truth. As You sent Me into the world, I also have sent them into the world. And for their sakes I sanctify Myself, that they also may be sanctified by the truth. I do not pray for these alone, but also for those who will believe in Me through their word; That they all may be one, as You, Father, are in Me, and I in You; that they also may be one in Us, that the world may believe that You sent Me. And the glory which You gave

Me I have given them, that they may be one just as We are one: I in them, and You in Me; that they may be made perfect in one, and that the world may know that You have sent Me, and have loved them as You have loved Me. John 17:13-23

Jesus prayed the Father's heart over the infant Church before she was birthed. His intercession prepared her for relationship. As He entered the finishing work of the cross, He opened the door of intimacy with the Father for everyone who would follow the Son. On the third day after His death, He arose to a new age of grace for all mankind. Out of the womb of that morning, the Church was birthed into the beauty of holiness.

You have the Dew of Your Youth

This infant Church was thrust into a world of chaos and persecution, but not without provision. Like a protective Father, Christ did not leave her alone and powerless. His last loving instructions guided His followers to their first encounter with their Holy Comforter and Counselor.

> *And being assembled together with them, He commanded them not to depart from Jerusalem, but to wait for the promise of the Father, "which," He said, "you have heard from Me; for John truly baptized with water, but you shall be baptized with the Holy Spirit not many days from now." Therefore, when they had come together, they asked Him, saying, "Lord, will You at this time restore the kingdom to Israel?" And He said to them, "It is not for you to know times or seasons which the Father has put in His own authority. But you shall receive power when the Holy Spirit has come upon you; and you shall be witnesses to Me in Jerusalem, and in all Judea and Samaria, and to the end of the earth."*
> *Acts 1:4-8*

After the Upper Room experience in Jerusalem, the newborn Church was complete in her relationship with the Triune God. Holy Spirit had come to nurture and empower her until the day when Jesus would return to claim His spotless Bride.

These disciples, who were born again by the power of the Holy Spirit, would literally go to the ends of the earth carrying the good news of the gospel of Jesus Christ. From one generation to another, their youthful strength and passion for Christ would be passed down until the return of their Savior King. Men who had previously abandoned their beloved

112

Teacher in His greatest hour of need would now become the scepter of His mighty love and power extended into a lost world.

The Holy Spirit transformed them from cowards into courageous volunteers who would literally lay down their own lives to display the glory of the King. These timid disciples turned away from dead religion and brought forth a living display of total devotion for the King of kings. They were raised up out of death into the life of the Living God.

From that encounter with the Holy Spirit in the upper room, these common men went forth with not only a message about the Messiah, but with an endowment of miraculous power given to them by the presence of Holy Spirit communing with them. They not only introduced the world to Jesus, the Son of God, but they also introduced mankind to the empowering Counselor and Comforter in the person of the Holy Spirit.

The disciples knew that the veil Jesus had opened for all mankind to encounter their heavenly Father also became the opportunity for them to be empowered and consoled by His Spirit. This Holy Spirit would enable them to live a life that would overcome the power of the enemies of the Living God. So, they carried the message of redemption and forgiveness, through Jesus, out into the world. And they also empowered those who accepted Jesus to live victoriously by introducing them to the presence and power of the Holy Spirit. This is what they proclaimed at Pentecost:

This Jesus God raised up, and of that all we [His disciples] are witnesses.... For David did not ascend into the heavens; yet he himself says, The Lord said to my Lord, Sit at My right hand and share My throne till I make Your enemies a footstool for Your feet...recognize beyond all doubt and acknowledge assuredly that God has made Him both Lord and Christ (the Messiah)— this Jesus Whom you crucified...Now when they heard this they were stung (cut) to the heart, and they said...Brethren, what shall we do? And Peter answered them, Repent...and be baptized...in the name of Jesus Christ for the forgiveness of and release from your sins; and you shall receive the gift of the Holy Spirit.... For the promise [of the Holy Spirit] is to and for you and your children, and to and for all that are far away, [even] to and for as many as the Lord our God invites and bids to come to Himself. Acts 2:32-29 (Amplified Bible)

The Completed Portrait

Pentecost was the final brushstroke of God painting His self-portrait for His newborn Church. The Holy Spirit was presented as a rushing wind and tongues of fire (Acts 2:1-4). What an entrance! And He continued to reveal Himself through Holy Spirit all through the New Testament. The infant Church now had a complete image of their Triune God. They could now carry His presence with them to the ends of the earth proclaiming His mercy and His might.

From this point forward the disciples presented the Holy Spirit as the consummation of a relationship with Father God and Jesus, His Son and their Redeemer. Jesus had already introduced the disciples to the necessity for them to be filled with the Holy Spirit's presence, but His appearance at Pentecost made them totally aware that His presence in their lives was the necessary element they needed to fully proclaim and live out the truth of Jesus as Messiah.

> *"And I will pray the Father, and He will give you another Helper, that He may abide with you forever—the Spirit of truth, whom the world cannot receive, because it neither sees Him nor knows Him; but you know Him, for He dwells with you and will be in you."*
>
> *John 14:16-17*

After Pentecost, the disciples went out carrying the message that Father God had sent Jesus His Son to redeem lives and fill them with His power through the indwelling presence of Holy Spirit. They proclaimed to the world that Jesus was the resurrected Son of God and Holy Spirit would empower them to live a resurrected life of faith in the Living Triune God.

Many people they encountered knew of the man Jesus and had believed him to be the Messiah, but few had heard of the Holy Spirit and their need to receive Him into their lives. Philip had been to Samaria and preached Christ to the people living there. Afterward many of them were baptized and learned of the kingdom of God. But later Peter and John went to meet with these people.

> ...they sent Peter and John to them, who, when they had come down, prayed for them that they might receive the Holy Spirit. For as yet He had fallen upon none of them. They had only been baptized in the name of the Lord Jesus. Then they laid hands on them, and they received the Holy Spirit. Acts 8:14-17

Later, Paul encountered believers of Jesus at Ephesus who knew nothing of the Holy Spirit.

> ...he said to them, "Did you receive the Holy Spirit when you believed?" So they said to him, "We have not so much as heard whether there is a Holy Spirit." And he said to them, "Into what then were you baptized?" So they said, "Into John's baptism." Then Paul said, John indeed baptized with a baptism of repentance, saying to the people that they should believe on Him who would come after him, that is, on Christ Jesus." When they heard this, they were baptized in the name of the Lord Jesus. And when Paul had laid hands on them, the Holy Spirit came upon them, and they spoke with tongues and prophesied. Acts 19:2-6

116

Whenever the Holy Spirit was presented to the people as a part of their vital belief in Jesus, they received Him and He manifested His presence powerfully in their lives. As the disciples learned at Pentecost, Holy Spirit was the power source they waited for so they could complete the assignment Jesus had given them to *"be witnesses to Me in Jerusalem, and in all Judea and Samaria, and to the end of the earth."* Acts 1:8

They did not hesitate to share this complete message of relationship with Father, Son and Holy Spirit to all who would listen. The results were astounding, enabling believers to continue sharing the life of Jesus down through the ages. And now, as then, it is necessary that the Church continue to be empowered by receiving the presence of the Holy Spirit into their midst to experience transformation, comfort and strength to continue the commission to

"Go therefore and make disciples of all the nations, baptizing them in the name of the Father and of the Son and of the Holy Spirit, teaching them to observe all things that I have commanded you."

Matthew 28: 19-20

God is still bringing forth a willing people, young and old, whose youth is renewed in His presence (Psalm 103:1-5 Amplified Bible). They are covering the earth like glistening dew in the morning sun, radiating the beauty of holiness. As you repent, accept forgiveness through the Lord Jesus Christ and receive the power of the Holy Spirit in your midst, you will be victorious over the enemies of Christ. As you daily

117

wait on God, enjoying His sweet communion, you will surely shine with His glory and become scepters of righteousness in His hand.

Now is the hour to be fully united with Almighty God—the Everlasting Father, the Prince of Peace and the Wonderful Counselor (Isaiah 9:6b). You must be actively involved with the movement of the Holy Spirit in the earth today. We all have different but definite assignments to carry out as a part of the Body of Christ on earth. No one is exempt. No one is left out of the responsibility to share the love of God and His holiness with the world around us. What a privilege to be a vital part of God's amazing plan to redeem all of creation for His kingdom and glory!

TODAY IS THE DAY

Today is the day of His grace,

Now is the time to seek His face.

Today brings a new opportunity.

Volunteer to live in His unity.

Today His beauty and power display,

Come join His army in holy array.

Today is the day of His grace

To thrive in your destiny place.

Questions for reflection:

When have you volunteered before the Lord to do something different than you normally do?

How did feel about your decision as you stepped fully into that place?

How is the Holy Spirit displaying His power through you to-day?

PSALM 110:4

The Lord has sworn and will not relent,
"You are a priest forever according to
the order of Melchizedek."

God gave His Word and
He won't take it back; you're (Jesus)
the permanent priest, the
melchizedech priest.

CHAPTER SEVEN

THE FATHER'S OATH

How good is your word? Most people with even a shred of integrity attempt to keep their word, especially if they have sworn to do it. Even in our courts of law, if you are called on to testify, you must swear, before the judge and jurors, to tell the whole truth. It is a serious commitment with serious consequences for misrepresenting the truth. Oaths are not to be taken lightly.

In David's culture a man was only as good as his word. A verbal oath was meant to be a permanent arrangement between two parties. The breaking of an oath could bring severe consequences, even death, to the man who did not keep his word. Unlike sinful mankind, the Lord has no trouble keeping His word.

God is not a man, that He should lie, nor a son of man, that He should repent. Has He said, and will He not do? Or has He spoken, and will He not make it good? Behold, I have received a command to bless; He has blessed, and I cannot reverse it. Numbers 23:19-20

This was the statement of Balaam the prophet. He knew he must follow the word of the Lord, because the Lord was always true to His word. When God makes an oath, He honors it. The prophet knew he could not bless those whom the Lord had cursed and could not curse those whom He blessed. No one can revoke God's oath.

David also knew the word of the Lord was the final authority on a matter. He expressed his belief in this fourth verse of Psalm 110. The Hebrew word for "sworn" in this passage actually means to be complete.[1] The Hebrew custom of swearing was to repeat a statement seven times. The number seven represents infinite fullness. Swearing in this manner was a sacred, irrevocable act.

As Jesus Christ sat down beside the Father on the throne, He became the High Priest of Heaven. In this verse, David recorded the irrevocable oath of the Father to His Son declaring His priesthood. The Father's adamant oath carried all His divine authority and power. There is no chance of revoke or change in the Father's decision. Jesus is the eternal Priest in the presence of the Father.

Through His life, death and resurrection, Jesus became our Priest. He became a priest after the order of Melchizedek. Melchizedek was the foreshadowing life of the eternal High Priest that would atone for the sin of mankind once and for all. The life of Melchizedek was a prophetic glimpse of Jesus, the Alpha and the Omega, the life with no beginning and no end.

The Significance of Melchizedek

In the history of Israel from the time of Moses until the time of Jesus, only Levites held the office of priest. When God originally established the priesthood for the people of Israel, He ordained Aaron, from the tribe of the Levites, to minister in the Tent of Meeting. From that time forward, only Levites could legitimately become priests in Israel.

However, about three centuries earlier, Abraham, the father of our faith and the nation of Israel, recognized a man called Melchizedek as the priest of God Most High. This man was the first person ever to minister in a priestly role before the Lord. Who was he and where did he come from? There is not much written in the Scripture about Melchizedek's life. But we will explore a few verses to get a better understanding of his relevance to the life of Jesus.

When Abraham brought back his nephew Lot from captivity, he encountered Melchizedek for the first time as a priest before God.

> *Then Melchizedek king of Salem brought out bread and wine; he was the priest of God Most High. And he blessed him and said: "Blessed be Abram of God Most High, Possessor of heaven and earth; and blessed be God Most High, Who has delivered your enemies into your hand." And he gave him a tithe of all. Genesis 14:18-21*

Melchizedek's name means king of righteousness. He was also the king of Salem, which is the modern day area of the city of Jerusalem. Salem means peace, thus, he was also the king of peace. He was a prophetic picture of Jesus Christ,

King of Righteousness and Prince of Peace. (See Hebrews 7:1-3)

Melchizedek also brought out bread and wine for Abraham. This act was a prophetic picture of the broken body and poured out blood of Christ.

> *And he took bread, and gave thanks, and brake it, and gave unto them, saying, "This is my body which is given for you: this do in remembrance of me." Likewise also the cup after supper, saying, "This cup is the new testament in my blood, which is shed for you." Luke 22:19-20 KJV*
>
> *And Jesus said to them, "I am the bread of life. He who comes to Me shall never hunger, and he who believes in Me shall never thirst. John 6:35*
>
> *I am the living bread which came down from heaven. If anyone eats of this bread, he will live forever; and the bread that I shall give is My flesh, which I shall give for the life of the world. John 6:51*

The ministry of Melchizedek to Abraham symbolized the provision of Father God to His covenant people. Father God provided the perfect sacrifice and nourishment for all who would worship Him through Jesus, the Son. Melchizedek recognized that God provided Abraham the victory over his enemies. And for those who follow God through a covenant relationship with Jesus Christ, victory over our enemies is sure.

Melchizedek was a king and acted as a priest before God for Abraham by receiving tithes and by blessing Abraham with bread and wine. David declares in this fourth verse

126

of Psalm 110 the irrevocable oath of the Father that Jesus is a priest after the same order as Melchizedek.

God revealed to David that the One seated at the right hand of the Father was the eternal King of Glory and High Priest of heaven and earth. This revelation given to David would defy all of Israel's knowledge of the priesthood. Jesus was not from the tribe of the Levites. He was a descendent of David who was of the tribe of Judah. God's oath to the Lord Jesus was not based on an earthly inheritance through an earthly bloodline. It was based on the broken body and poured out blood of Jesus Himself. His obedience unto death through His intimate relationship with God the Father paved the way for Him to be declared the High Priest of Heaven and the King of kings. And this declaration would confirm, to the generations who came after the birth of Jesus, that the nature of the priestly role had changed.

Therefore, David became a prophetic voice declaring this new order of the priesthood yet to come. He ushered it into earth's realm through his obedient recording of God's word and vision. David saw in the heavenly realms of His God what was to come, and then, through his declaration, opened the door of revelation on earth for God's oath to be fulfilled in Jesus.

Confirming Words

The prophet Zechariah confirms this revelation that Jesus is indeed King and Priest, ordained by God to build the true temple of the Lord:

Thus says the Lord of hosts: [You, Joshua] behold (look at, keep in sight, watch) the Man [the Messiah] whose name is the Branch, for He shall grow up in His place and He shall build the [true] temple of the Lord. Yes, [you are building a temple of the Lord, but] it is He Who shall build the [true] temple of the Lord, and He shall bear the honor and glory [as of the only begotten of the Father] and shall sit and rule upon His throne, and the counsel of peace shall be between the two [offices—Priest and King].   Zechariah 6:13 (Amplified Bible)

The apostle John declared to the churches:

Grace to you and peace from Him who is and who was and who is to come, and from the seven Spirits who are before His throne, and from Jesus Christ, the faithful witness, the firstborn from the dead, and the ruler over the kings of the earth. To Him who loved us and washed us from our sins in His own blood, and has made us kings and priests to His God and Father, to Him be glory and dominion forever and ever. Amen. Revelation 1:4-6

John also records the new song being sung in heaven about the Lamb of God (Jesus) and the people He has redeemed:

"You are worthy to take the scroll,

And to open its seals;

For You were slain,

And have redeemed us to God by Your blood

Out of every tribe and tongue and people and nation,

And have made us kings and priests to our God;

And we shall reign on the earth."

Revelation 5:9-10

David, Zechariah and John all received heavenly visions of the Kingdom Jesus was building as King and Priest before God. As a follower of Jesus Christ, you are also a king and a priest. You have authority and power from God to bring His holy nature and government into earth's realm. As you walk and live intimately united with Jesus, who sits at the right hand of the Father, you can execute His government and peace through your own intercession and witness.

God's government and peace is to increase on earth through the people who bow before Jesus. As He raises them up from darkness into light, they will sit beside Him and the Father in intimacy, receiving truth and power to speak and act as scepters of His righteousness.

For unto us a Child is born, unto us a Son is given; and the government will be upon His shoulder. And His name will be called Wonderful, Counselor, Mighty God, Everlasting Father, Prince of Peace. Of the increase of His government and peace there will be no end, upon the throne of David and over His kingdom, to order it and establish it with judgment and justice from that time forward, even forever. The zeal of the Lord of hosts will perform this. Isaiah 9:6-8

The writer of the New Testament book of Hebrews gives an excellent commentary in chapters five and seven on this eternal oath of the Father and the new unchangeable priesthood of Christ.

While he lived on earth, anticipating death, Jesus cried out in pain and wept in sorrow as he offered up priestly prayers to God. Because he honored God, God answered him. Though he was God's Son, he learned trusting-obedience by what he suffered, just as we do. Then, having arrived at the full stature of his maturity and having been announced by God as high priest in the order of Melchizedek, he became the source of eternal salvation to all who believingly obey him. Hebrews 5:7-10 (The Message)

So now we have a high priest who perfectly fits our needs: completely holy, uncompromised by sin, with authority extending as high as God's presence in heaven itself. Unlike the other high priests, he doesn't have to offer sacrifices for his own sins every day before he can get around to us and our sins. He's done it, once and for all: offered up himself as the sacrifice. The law appoints as high priests men who are never able to get the job done right. But this intervening command of God, which came later, appoints the Son, who is absolutely, eternally perfect. Hebrews 7:26-28 (The Message)

Now, every willing person can enter into a new covenant with God through the perfect and eternal High Priest who

130

sits at the right hand of Father God interceding for us continually. The covenant of the Old Testament is fulfilled in Jesus. The Covenant Maker Himself has provided a new and living way into His presence. Jesus has become our High Priest.

The priests of the Old Covenant had no power to offer an eternally perfect sacrifice. They were limited, with only the imperfect blood of animals for sacrifice. But the Perfect One came as a living sacrifice to atone for mankind once and for all. You no longer have to be slaves to sin and the enemy. You have been given the freedom to choose to be children of the Most High God. All the benefits of the family inheritance of eternal life in Christ Jesus can be yours.

There is a New Covenant by which you have access to the Father. Who could ask for a better arrangement? This change in covenant can never be revoked or altered because the Lord of Creation has personally ordained it and will honor His word—His Living Word. God's word is truth and He does not lie or repent!

Benefits of the New Priestly Order

How does this new priestly order affect your life? There are a host of eternal benefits for those who come to Jesus Christ, the High Priest of Heaven. Jesus fulfills this position like no human Levitical priest ever could. He sits at the right hand of the Father God as an equal—perfect and holy. He provides amazing and abundant assets you don't even know you need.

Advocacy

Jesus's life, death and resurrection completed the necessary atoning sacrifice needed to satisfy the Father's wrath against sin. And He sits beside the Living God as an eternal advocate for every born-again believer. He intercedes for you continually before the Father to bring you into right relationship and maturity with Him. (I John 2:1-2)

If you have received Jesus as your Savior and then discover that you have sinned against God through your attitudes or behavior, Jesus acts as your advocate (lawyer) before the Father. When you repent, Jesus presents your case for mercy because His blood has already covered that sin and you have recognized your need for forgiveness.

I believe Jesus is also continually interceding for you with the Father, so that you may be assisted by the Holy Spirit to come out of any darkness remaining in your soul and into the fullness of His marvelous light. (Hebrews 7:25)

Complete Redemption

Jesus brought His own pure blood into the Holy of Holies and secured your complete redemption for all of eternity. (Hebrews 9:12) The blood of animals was not sufficient to bring eternal redemption from sin. It had to be offered again and again for men to be made pure in God's eyes. But the one-time application of the blood of Jesus in the Holy of Holies was sufficient for God to grant mercy to all those who live in relationship with Him through faith in Jesus Christ.

Justification

By the merciful grace of God, you are justified by your faith in the atoning blood of Jesus Christ. You are cleansed by His life-giving sacrifice and made righteous in the eyes of the Father. Your acts do not make you righteous, but they will reflect your righteousness as you act in obedience to God's word. Your faith in the righteousness of Jesus is what causes the Father to pardon your sin without demanding punishment. You are freed from the demand of the law and declared righteous because of your faith in the Righteous Redeemer. (Romans 3:21-26)

Newness of Life

Jesus provides new life to each person who trusts Him. He makes you a new creature, alive unto God. (2 Corinthians 5:17) I was raised in a Christian home and grew up going to church often. My parents trained me to live a moral life. I joined the church when I was in elementary school, but I don't think I really came to know the Lord as my personal savior until I was in high school.

I joined a Young Life club that met weekly in the homes of fellow students. The gospel was presented to me as a very personal and intimate relationship with the Lord. I said the sinner's prayer at a weekend retreat and felt a new presence and power within that changed my thinking.

Before that time, I was conscious of pleasing my parents, my teachers and my peers. My motivation to be "good" was the acceptance of those who were near and dear to me. But after the experience on the weekend retreat, I felt that Jesus was the one I needed to please. I didn't always stay on track with that revelation in my choices. But when I did make a choice that was not God's will for my life, I could definitely feel the conviction and power of God's presence to change my thinking and confess my sins.

Before, I could hide things from my parents and leaders, but now that Jesus had become my Savior, I could not hide anything from Him and I felt His conviction strongly. I began to make my choices according to His desire and not my own desire or the desires of those around me. Every time I drifted away from close fellowship with Him, that feeling of deep remorse and the wooing of His love would pull me back into His presence once again. I could not escape the fact that I could no longer live for myself or other people, but only for His pleasure and satisfaction.

Sometimes the choices have been hard, but as I have followed Him, He always makes them worthwhile for me. I can truly say I became a new person with new motives, desires, peace and love. He continues to lead me into deeper experiences of His goodness and greatness every day. Life with Jesus is not boring!!

Reconciliation *#1 ministry*

You are reconciled to the Father by the intercession of Jesus Christ before the Throne of Heaven. You are brought into harmony with your Creator and given a ministry of reconciliation to influence the lives of others. (1 Corinthians 5:18) When you accept Jesus as your Savior, you are no longer estranged from the Father's heart by your sin. He fully embraces you as His child, created by His own design. Sin no longer blocks the blessings He desires to bestow on you and the lines of communication are fully opened for you to intimately come to know Him as a member of the family of God. There is no distance or barrier between you and Father, Son or Holy Spirit. You have access to all the richness of the Kingdom of God.

Freedom from Condemnation

With Jesus as your High Priest, there is no longer anyone to condemn you before the Father. His continual intercession provides the bridge you need to be ever present in the Father's love. (Romans 8:1-2, 33-35) If you do sin, the conviction of God comes to rescue you from the dangerous trap of living in that sin and reaping the death it brings. Conviction does not come in a condemning, degrading voice, but in the firm, loving, convincing power of the Holy Spirit to warn you and draw you back to the place of peace and rest in God.

Repentance quickly restores your communion with God. He puts the sin behind Him and quickly forgets you were ever engaged in it. He immediately moves forward and does not continually remind you of your failure. He seeks to build you up, not put you down. The enemy of your soul is the one who continually reminds you of past failures. Your Father reminds you that you were bought with a priceless sacrifice and you are valuable and acceptable to Him. You are free to be who He created you to be.

Uttermost Salvation

The eternal intercession of Jesus, the High Priest, provides a complete and eternal salvation for you. This salvation begins with your first bow at the feet of Jesus and continues into eternity as you continually submit yourself to His will and enjoy His presence. (Hebrews 7:22-25) Jesus is interceding for you so that you receive **all** the benefits of living in God's presence and fulfill **all** the plans and purposes you were created for. His desire is for you to be completely restored to the original creative design of the Father, Son and Holy Spirit as they conceived your life and brought you forth into the world. Full and complete life is available to each of us as we continue to live and grow in fellowship with our God. Salvation is not just an escape from the pit of hell, but fullness of life here and now and forever!

These are just a few of the eternal benefits of the new priestly order in Christ Jesus. How comforting and encouraging is it to know that you are continually covered by the prayers of the Son of Father God? As you abide in the presence of Jesus through worship and prayer, you need not fear being left alone and uncovered. God's provision for His children is amazing and reassuring. Praise God, His word is irrevocable!

The New Order Begins

We can observe the priestly ministry of Jesus on earth as He was preparing to go to the cross. John 17:6-19 records Jesus's priestly prayer for His disciples. As He turned His attention to His Father in Heaven, He lifted up His dear friends before the Throne of Heaven. His desire was for them to have the same knowledge and glory He had with the Father. Even though they made many mistakes and would soon forsake Him in His hour of sacrifice, His heart was to connect them with His Father.

> *I have manifested Your name to the men whom You have given Me out of the world. They were Yours, You gave them to Me, and they have kept Your word. Now they have known that all things which You have given Me are from You...I pray for them. I do not pray for the world but for those whom You have given Me, for they are Yours. I do not pray that You should take them out of the world, but that You should keep them from the evil one...Sanctify them by Your truth. Your word is truth... And for their sakes I sanctify Myself, that they also may be sanctified by the truth. John 17:6-19*

His prayer did not end with the disciples. He also interceded for all those who would ever come to know Him and the power of His resurrection. He stood in the gap for all the believers yet to be born in all the generations to come.

> *I do not pray for these alone, but also for those who will believe in Me through their word; that they all may be one, as You, Father, are in Me, and I in You; that they also may be one in Us, that the world may believe that You sent Me...O righteous Father! The world has*

> *not known You, but I have known You; and these have known that You sent Me. And I have declared to them Your name, and will declare it, that the love with which You loved Me may be in them, and I in them. John 17:20-26*

You have such a glorious High Priest in Christ Jesus! He alone is perfect, holy and worthy to stand before the Father on your behalf. He is the only priest you need in order to have a right relationship with your Creator. The Father has ordained Him and *the Lord has sworn and will not relent!*

> *...for You were slain (sacrificed), and with Your blood You purchased men unto God from every tribe and language and people and nation. And You have made them a kingdom (royal race) and priests to our God, and they shall reign [as kings] over the earth! Revelation 5:9-10 (Amplified Bible)*

As a disciple of Christ, you can carry God's government and peace into your family, your neighborhood, your city, your country and to the ends of the earth. You are able to pray the priestly prayers of Jesus and carry His authority declaring His will in the earth as He inspires and equips you. Holy Spirit will lead and guide you to expand the Kingdom of God everywhere you put your feet if you take time to linger before Him in worship and prayer, becoming a resting place for His presence.

Remember, the Lord provided His salvation to restore all of mankind to the original state of His creation before the fall. You were created to rule and reign with Him. You were created to carry the thoughts and intents of His heart. And

138

through the precious blood of Jesus, you have been given a way to access the resources of heaven, to live in His kingdom as a priest and a king while you live on earth. This privilege and responsibility is not for later in the sweet by and by, but for now as you walk and move throughout your life. You were created to bring forth His resurrection life into the atmosphere around you. It is your calling and your inheritance as a child of God!

PRAYER

Father, thank You for the assurance of Your irrevocable word declaring Jesus to be my Priest. I am so grateful to know that He continually intercedes for me before Your throne, even when I am not aware of my own need. Thank You for the revelation of His kingship over the earth. Help me to receive His power to reign where I live with His great humility and grace. This promise to Your Son brings me great peace and confidence in Your loving plan for my life to live as a king and priest in Your Kingdom while I live on earth. In the unchangeable name of Jesus, I praise You!

Questions for reflection:

What has the Holy Spirit shown you in God's word or in prayer that may be quite different than your family traditions or your early understanding of God and His ways?

How do you relate to Jesus as your priest before Father God?

How do you see yourself acting as a priest and a king with godly authority in your realm of influence?

PSALM 110:5-6

The Lord is at Your right hand;
He shall execute kings in the
day of His wrath.
He shall judge among the nations,
He shall fill the places with dead bodies,
He shall execute the heads of many countries.

CHAPTER EIGHT

THE RIGHTEOUS JUDGE

In the first few verses of Psalm 110, David shared a glimpse of the righteous compassion and grace that Jesus ushered into the earth through His birth, life, death and resurrection. He paid the price for our sin and made a way for us to escape the wrath of God and enter His kingdom as sons and daughters to become kings and priests. Through His broken body and poured out blood, those who repent and believe on Him as Savior and Lord become one with Him by the indwelling power of the Holy Spirit. They become His Body on the earth, carrying His love and authority wherever He leads them.

That amazing and powerful process is still going on today. The kingdom of God is expanding and moving all across this earth. The door is still open to people in every nation to come into the family of God and be a vital part of His Body in the earth.

However, in these next two verses of Psalm 110, you will see a different facet of Jesus's authority and power. He is described as the one who will judge the nations and execute kings and leaders. These verses speak of the *day of His wrath.* Again, the Hebrew word for day is indicative of an age or period of time. This day of His wrath is the age in which the doors for change will be closed and mankind will be judged and rewarded according to their choice for or against Christ.

When the prophet Isaiah declared the birth of the Son of God, he spoke of the everlasting increase of the government of God upon the earth through Jesus. The Father, Son and Holy Spirit are continually working through the lives of believers to increase His righteous authority and abundant peace in individuals and in nations. (Isaiah 9:6-7)

The apostle Paul spoke to the Corinthian believers of the coming time when the enemies of God would be subdued by the Living God.

For He must reign till He has put all enemies under His feet. The last enemy that will be destroyed is death. For "He has put all things under His feet." 1 Corinthians 15:25-26

The writer of the book of Hebrews referred to this Psalm when he spoke of the permanent rule of God over His creation.

But to the Son He says: "Your throne, O God, is forever and ever; a scepter of righteousness is the scepter of Your kingdom. You have loved righteousness and hated lawlessness; therefore God, Your God, has anointed You with the oil of gladness more than Your companions." And: "You, Lord, in the beginning laid the foundation of the earth, and the heavens are the work of Your hands. They will perish, but You remain; and they will all grow old like a garment; like a cloak You will fold them up, and they will be changed. But You are the same, and Your years will not fail." But to which of the angels has He ever said: "Sit at My right hand, till I make Your enemies Your footstool"? Hebrews 1:8-13

These scriptures point to the everlasting and increasing reign of the risen King of Glory, Jesus Christ. They also remind you that, through God's judgment and justice, His reign will be established and ordered and will continue eternally. Not only is Jesus Christ the Savior and Priest of His creation, but as King, He is the Judge who will execute righteousness in the earth.

The Law of Perfect Judgment

As you study these particular verses, a thread of doubt could easily creep into your mind, causing you to question the mercy and compassion of this God who would "fill the places with dead bodies" and "execute heads of many countries." But this same God who promises to make His enemies the footstool of His Son is the same God who sent His beloved only Son to die as a sacrifice to cover the sin of every person on earth. Father provided the perfect sacrifice to appease His own wrath against sin. How merciful is His heart!

When thinking on the contrast between God's mercy and His justice, I thought of the law of gravity at work in the earth. Gravity holds the inhabitants and resources of the earth in place as our planet spins through space. It is a merciful force that keeps us anchored and safe.

On the other hand, gravity can cause your death if you try to defy it. You cannot leap from a tall building and escape the force of gravity. The same force that holds you here in safety can kill you if you don't respect the intent of the law itself. Gravity is meant to be a safety feature, but if disregarded and ignored, it can be deadly.

Gravity is designed to be a keeper of life, but it becomes a killer when you choose to live outside its boundaries. So is the nature of God's laws. They are meant to preserve the righteousness and holiness in which creation thrives. But for those who live contrary to this perfect plan of life eternal, their actions can bring destruction or death.

God, in His infinite mercy and grace, has done everything necessary to bring this lost creation into a loving relationship with Him. For centuries, He has poured Himself out in unselfish, unconditional love to reveal His true heart for all mankind, the crown of His creation. You were created in His image to live in fellowship with Him, enjoying His love and truth and sharing the responsibility of managing His kingdom on earth.

This perfectly merciful God is also perfectly just. He weighs the heart of each individual by their response to His gift of love and redemption through Jesus Christ. Those who reject the Son of His love have rejected the God of love Himself. The consequences of God's judgments are chosen by each person as they choose their way in life.

> *Even the Father judges no one, for He has given all judgment (the last judgment and the whole business of judging) entirely into the hands of the Son...I assure you, most solemnly I tell you, the person whose ears are open to My words [who listens to My message] and believes and trusts in and clings to and relies on Him Who sent Me has (possesses now) eternal life. And he does not come into judgment [does not incur sentence of judgment, will not come under condemnation], but he has already passed over out of death into life. John 5:22-24 (Amplified Bible)*

Just as God's love and mercy has been poured out in overwhelming abundance, so will His justice be poured out on those who reject His Son. His perfect mercy is matched by His perfect justice. This generous gift of love cannot be ignored without generous consequence. His majesty is seated in love, even as His justice falls upon those who despise and reject His merciful outpouring of grace.

147

Just as death or injury is the result of ignoring gravity, so death and destruction come to those who ignore God's mercy and compassion offered through faith in Jesus Christ. There is no true life without the Creator of Life. Life comes through no other source. To choose relationship with God is to choose life. Life without that relationship leads to destruction and eternal death.

Created to Rule

Our Father God is a family man. He invented family. He has modeled family in His relationship with His creation and with Jesus, His Son. He prepared a dwelling place of abundance and joy in His original design of earth. The Garden of Eden was a paradise with all things provided for the enjoyment and development of man. There God offered protection and provision for man and woman to *"be fruitful and multiply; fill the earth and subdue it; have dominion...."* Genesis 1:28

The Father provided a perfect environment for man to continue to be the image of God in the realm of earth. God blessed man and woman to continue the legacy of providing for and protecting their children and ruling the garden to maintain the order and sufficiency of His original design.

Only one command came along with that extravagant provision:

> *Of every tree of the garden you may freely eat; but of the tree of the knowledge of good and evil you shall not eat, for in the day that you eat of it you shall surely die." Genesis 2:16-17*

With that command, the power of choice was given to man. God gave man the power to choose between life and death. He was warning them that only He has the ability to discern good from evil. He is the Creator and He alone is able to see the beginning from the end. He alone knew the danger that this knowledge tree held for man. God was asking man to trust His wisdom and follow in His footsteps of creating and ruling according to His sovereign design. He was enabling

149

man to reflect His glory, but asking man to trust Him alone for life.

God wanted man to know Him as Father, but He also wanted man to know Him as Ruler. God is both, not either-or. He is relational and He is sovereign. He desires to be present with us, but He can stand alone, complete and lacking nothing. He wants man to rule alongside Him, but He will not be ruled over. He is I AM—the Alpha and the Omega.

As a child of God, you are called to be a disciple of Christ, the **perfect** Son of God. Jesus is your model for being God's child. Jesus reigned in the extravagance of heaven alongside the Father. But He volunteered to leave the comfort and privilege of the throne to come to earth and redeem creation back into the dominion and care of the Father. He used His power of choice to sacrifice Himself for the reconciliation of all mankind to the Father's heart.

As a child of God, you are called to a place of maturity and sacrifice. Father God has tenderly provided all you need for life and godliness (1 Peter 1:1-8). He desires for you to prosper in your soul and surroundings so you can turn and pour out the blessings of His provision into the lives of those around you. Your faith in Father God should be leading you into the brotherly love of Christ, enabling you to become a minister of reconciliation.

Now all things are of God, who has reconciled us to Himself through Jesus Christ, and has given us the ministry of reconciliation...and has committed to us the word of reconciliation. 2 Corinthians 5:18-19

Whatever you receive from the Lord, you are commissioned to pass it on to others, just as Jesus did. He did on earth whatever He saw the Father doing in heaven. He lived a life of submission to the Father as a man on earth.

> *I can of Myself do nothing. As I hear, I judge; and My judgment is righteous, because I do not seek My own will but the will of the Father Who sent Me. John 5:30*

The judgments Jesus made on earth came directly from the heart of the Father in heaven. The Father delighted in the judgments Jesus made while He was on earth. He delighted in hearing Jesus declare what the Father had intimately shared with Him as they communed in prayer. Before Jesus began His earthly ministry, He went to John the Baptist to be baptized. The Father declared His delight in His Son as He arose from the waters:

> *And when Jesus was baptized, He went up at once out of the water; and behold, the heavens were opened and he [John] saw the Spirit of God descending like a dove and alighting on Him. And behold, a voice from heaven said, "This is my Son, My beloved, in Whom I delight!" Matthew 3:16-17 (Amplified Bible)*

David prophesied this declaration of the Father in Psalm 2, as he speaks about the kings of the earth and their foolishness in defying the "Anointed One:"

> *The kings of the earth set themselves, and the rulers take counsel together, against the Lord and against His Anointed...*

151

> *"Yet I have set My King on My holy hill of Zion. I will declare the decree: The Lord has said to Me, 'You are My Son, today I have begotten You. Ask of Me, and I will give You the nations for Your inheritance, and the ends of the earth for Your possession.'"...*
>
> *Now therefore, be wise, O kings; be instructed, you judges of the earth. Serve the Lord with fear and rejoice with trembling. Kiss the Son, lest He be angry, and you perish in the way, when His wrath is kindled but a little. Blessed are all those who put their trust in Him.*

David saw the heart of the Father and His delight in His righteous Son and declared the intentions of the Father to give Him the earth as His inheritance. The warning of wrath came to any earthly ruler that would try to defy the Son's right to rule the nations. The arrogance and pride in evil leaders will meet the divine justice of the Son of the Living God.

Bringing the Rule of Heaven on Earth

Isaiah also made a declaration of the Father's delight in the Son and His mandate to establish the justice of God in the earth:

> *Behold My Servant, Whom I uphold, My elect in Whom My soul delights! I have put My Spirit upon Him; He will bring forth justice and right and reveal truth to the nations.... He will bring forth justice in truth.... He will not fail or become weak or be crushed and discouraged till He has established justice in the earth.... Isaiah 42:1-4 (Amplified Bible)*

Jesus ruled and reigned at the right hand of the Father before the foundations of earth were laid. He continued to rule and reign on earth even as He brought the message of reconciliation with the Father to the hearts of men and women. As He displayed the message of hope and restoration through signs and miracles and taught the truth to all who would listen, He was challenged continually by the hierarchy of the Jewish leaders. They questioned His wisdom and judgment because He seemed to defy the Law of Moses. They did not understand that Jesus came to fulfill the Law not just talk about it and demand obedience to it.

The religious leaders criticized Jesus for healing a man on the Sabbath because they considered that to be work and, thereby, He was breaking the Law of Moses. His answer made them furious because they used the Law to rule over others. His answer to them revealed His mandate as Judge.

But Jesus answered them, "My Father has been working until now, and I have been working....

"For the Father loves the Son, and shows Him all things that He Himself does; and He will show Him greater works than these, that you may marvel....

"For as the Father raises the dead and gives life to them, even so the Son gives life to whom He will....

"For the Father judges no one, but has committed all judgment to the Son....

"and has given Him authority to execute judgment also, because He is the Son of Man." John 5:17-27

Jesus knew how to follow the lead of the Father as He walked on the earth, teaching, doing miracles and making judgments. He submitted Himself to the wisdom of God because He was a man in the flesh. He is our example in following, listening to and obeying the Father's heart as a son.

When Philip asked Jesus to show them (the twelve disciples) the Father, Jesus gave this answer:

"Have I been with you so long, and yet you have not known Me, Philip? He who has seen Me has seen the Father; so how can you say, 'Show us the Father'?

"Do you not believe that I am in the Father, and the Father in Me? The words that I speak to you I do not speak on My own authority; but the Father who dwells in Me does the works.

"Believe Me that I am in the Father and the Father in Me, or else believe Me for the sake of the works themselves.

> *"Most assuredly, I say to you, he who believes in Me, the works that I do he will do also; and greater works than these he will do, because I go to My Father.*
>
> *"And whatever you ask in My name, that I will do, that the Father may be glorified in the Son." John 14:8-13*

Jesus ruled beside the Father before the world was created. He ruled beside the Father when man fell into sin in the Garden. He ruled with the Father when He walked the earth as a man. He rules now at the right hand of the Father on the throne of heaven. As King of kings, He is the righteous judge of all creation. The Father has given Him all authority in heaven and earth to rule and judge righteously.

You are called, as a disciple, to live the same kind of life that Jesus did in your own realm of influence on the earth. You are called to sit at the feet of the Father, listening for His heartbeat, watching His moves of compassion, observing His righteous judgments against evil. You are called to wait for His specific instructions to express what you are seeing and hearing in the throne room through strategic prayer and action on the earth.

Jesus knew, by the power of the Holy Spirit, when to speak a word of compassion and encouragement, a word of correction and instruction, or a word of judgment on those who perpetrated evil and corruption. He healed and delivered, but He also disrupted and judged the practitioners of oppression and deception. He knew how to judge the unjust and when to extend mercy to the oppressed.

You are also called by the Father, through the power of the Holy Spirit, to deliver His mercy toward those that are oppressed and weary, and to discern His righteous judgments toward evil and corruption. Neither of these actions should be entered into with a flippant or arrogant attitude. Neither of these actions should be executed without a pure heart toward God and the people you are called to reach. Emotion or logic cannot be the force behind the action. These works must be led and controlled by the Spirit of God, not the soul of man. Both of these works can be corrupted by impure motives.

To Judge or Not to Judge?

When you begin to contemplate the possibility that God may ask you to deliver a word of correction or a warning of impending judgment to a person, a city or a nation, the fear of God should be the attitude of your heart. Such words of correction and warning are meant to bring the hearer into a place of accountability toward their Creator. The motive in God's heart is to bring men to repentance and out of destruction. That should be your motive as well.

As you enter into deeper relationship with Father, Son and Holy Spirit, you are called to a place of maturity that will equip you to seek the souls of men for the pleasure of the Father and the glory of the Son. You become equipped with the power of Holy Spirit to speak the truth in love and boldness.

The apostle, John, makes a challenging statement concerning our position before God in this hour:

> *Love has been perfected among us in this: that we may have boldness in the day of judgment; because as He is, so are we in this world. 1 John 4:17*

When you are walking with the Lord in His perfect love, you are to have boldness to move and speak as He does. We live in a period of time in which the choices of men are putting them under God's protection and blessing or putting them in the precarious place of separation from God eternally.

This scripture is in the present tense: *as He is, so are we in this world.* Jesus is now at the right hand of the Father and that is where you need to be. The Church must be spending time at the Father's side, learning, observing and imitating the ministry of Jesus. He is boldly interceding for the saints and the lost. He is boldly declaring words of wisdom and warning regarding the actions of men.

As you are interceding through prayer and speaking into the lives of those around you, you should be speaking His bold words of healing, encouragement, correction and possibly warning into the lives of those He brings into your presence. You are to be about the business of bringing the kingdom of God to earth. You are to be preparing a way for His triumphant return.

You are to be bringing others into His forgiving presence and equipping them to stand with you against the evil plots and plans of His enemies, both natural and spiritual. Evil people who inflict pain and suffering on others should be confronted with the truth of their fate before God. And evil spirits that fuel those people should be confronted with God's word through prayer and declaration. Holy Spirit may direct you to engage either or both of these enemies.

Paul spoke of his mandate to preach the Gospel to the Gentiles and bring the Church into their place of power and anointing:

*...I should preach among the Gentiles the unsearchable riches of Christ, and to make all to see what is the fellowship of the mystery, which from the beginning of the ages has been hidden in God who created all things through Jesus Christ; to the intent that **now** the manifest wisdom of God might be made known **by the church** to the principalities and powers in the heavenly places, according to the eternal purpose which He accomplished in Christ Jesus our Lord, **in whom we have***

158

boldness and access with confidence through faith in Him. Ephesians 3:8-12 (emphasis mine)

The Church will make known to powers in the heavenly places, through prayer and declarations, what the wisdom of God is for this hour. Your mandate is to change the atmosphere and confront the evil and corruption that fuels the unredeemed hearts of men. You can be setting the stage, through prayer and practice, for all men to be able to freely choose the loving redemption of God.

Not all will choose wisely, but without a model and an atmosphere of God's presence, many will be lost. The Church is to be the model and set the atmosphere of intimacy and boldness through faith and confidence in God's love and favor.

*He raised Him from the dead and seated Him at His right hand in the heavenly places, far above all principality and power and might and dominion, and every name that is named, not only in this age but also in that which is to come. **And He put all things under His feet, and gave Him to be head over all things to the church, which is His body, the fullness of Him who fills all in all.** Ephesians 1:20-23 (emphasis mine)*

Jesus is the head and the Church is the body of Christ in the earth. He rules and the Church is to carry out that ruling in the earth as He directs. The Church is to be carrying out the redemptive plan of bringing the Kingdom of heaven to earth. The Message version of this same verse really puts an interesting light on the role of the Church.

All this energy issues from Christ: God raised him from death and set him on a throne in deep heaven, in charge of running the universe, everything from galaxies to governments, no name and no power exempt from his rule. And not just for the time being, but forever. He is in charge of it all, has the final word on everything. At the center of all this, Christ rules the church. The church, you see, is not peripheral to the world; the world is peripheral to the church. The church is Christ's body, in which he speaks and acts, by which he fills everything with his presence. Ephesians 1:20-23 (The Message)

Do you see this happening in our world today? Is the Church actually at the center of governments and galaxies? Is the Church the reigning influence of society where you live? Is the Church influencing every aspect of your culture: family, religion, government, arts, business, medicine, education? Is the Church at the center of activity on this earth?

The Church has been given the power and the authority to be the leading and prevailing influence in our world. God has made full provision for His people to step up and live in His wisdom, compassion and uncompromising authority. The Church is called to walk as Jesus did and judge as Jesus did and still does.

When the hearts of believers are knit together in intimacy with God in prayer and practice, the tides of evil and corruption will have to change. Unrighteousness will have to bow to the righteousness of God in Christ Jesus as modeled by the Church.

What Did Jesus Say?

All this talk about judging seems to fly in the face of the very words of Jesus Himself. This very familiar scripture comes immediately to mind as we think along the lines of judgment.

> *Do not judge and criticize and condemn others, so that you may not be judged and criticized and condemned yourselves. For just as you judge and criticize and condemn others, it will be dealt out again to you. Matthew 7:1-2 (Amplified Bible)*

I believe Jesus was talking here of the attitudes behind our words and actions. Certainly we all must make judgments or discern, according to the knowledge we have, between what is right and just and what is wrong for us as children of God. We all have to decide for ourselves what is the best word to speak, decision to make and way to walk in our lives.

We have civil laws in place in our communities and even in our homes to protect the innocent from the evil and unjust practices of others. Those boundaries are in place to promote safety and welfare for all, not just a few.

I believe the Lord was speaking of the attitude and intent of our heart as we make judgments in our lives. Are we just criticizing another's actions to be complaining and malicious, or are we looking for a way to lead them into a more righteous path of living for their own benefit and the benefit of those around them?

He explains his statement in the verses following His admonition not to judge:

161

Or how can you say to your brother, Let me get the tiny particle out of your eye, when there is the beam of timber in your own eye? You hypocrite, first get the beam of timber out of your own eye, and then you will see clearly to take the tiny particle out of your brother's eye. Matthew 7:4-5

I believe Jesus meant for us to make sure our own hearts were free of condemnation and hate towards others as we observe their choices in life. All of us have made choices contrary to the will and desire of God. We often make choices that are totally selfish and cause others pain or suffering. But I believe it is our Father's desire for us to see others in the light of His love and wisdom. Our intent and attitude should come from pure hearts that desire to assist others to choose His words and ways for their lives. Our hearts must first be free of sin and selfish motives before we can offer words of correction or direction for others.

Even if you have no voice in another's life, you can affect them and their circumstances by praying from the heart of God. It is He alone that makes the final decision over a life for mercy or justice. Our job is to hear His words to us as how we are to speak and pray over the life of another. Our opinions are not important, but His word holds supreme value and authority. It is His word on a matter that will bring forth life and justice.

The Hour of Choice

Moreover the law entered that the offense might abound. But where sin abounded, grace abounded much more, so that as sin reigned in death, even so grace might reign through righteousness to eternal life through Jesus Christ our Lord. Romans 5:20

Even as men are choosing to reject the gift of life through faith in Jesus Christ, God is still pouring out His generous grace to all mankind. The choice between mercy and wrath is made by each individual throughout his lifetime. Each new moment is an opportunity to choose life over destruction.

We are all promised opportunity to choose. However, there is no promise concerning the number of moments we will have for choosing. Each hour spent on earth is an opportunity to choose everlasting life over eternal separation from God. As long as you have breath, the choice is yours to make. God is truly merciful toward His creation as He offers everyone time to choose Him.

Now is the time to make certain you are rightly positioned before the Throne of the Living God. Are you bowing in adoration and reverence or resisting the inevitable victory of the Son of God over all His enemies?

Now is the time for every believer to join in the intercessions of Christ Jesus for the harvest of the nations of the earth. Eventually, His wrath will be fully unleashed and manifested against all unrighteousness.

Now is the time to model the life of Christ through great acts of love and faith.

Now is the time for us to stand for righteousness in the face of fear and persecution. The world must see the reflection of the King of Glory in the earth. All, who believe in and confess Him as Lord and Savior, are called to reflect His glory in this hour.

Even as I write these words, a cry rises from my heart, "But God, how will we do it? How will these weak bodies of flesh ever measure up to the task of this hour?" So many times we try to do the things the Lord has called us to from a place of human effort instead of by the leading of His Spirit. We get anxious and try to carry out the responsibilities of the kingdom through the strength of familiar religious patterns of work and behavior. The result most often brings frustration and wears out our minds and bodies. But the Lord has a better way.

"Are you tired? Worn out? Burned out on religion? Come to me. Get away with me and you'll recover your life. I'll show you how to take a real rest. Walk with me and work with me—watch how I do it. Learn the unforced rhythms of grace. I won't lay anything heavy or ill-fitting on you. Keep company with me and you'll learn to live freely and lightly." Matthew 11:28-30 (The Message)

This encouraging word from the Lord Jesus offers great hope in the face of a world tottering on the brink of unprecedented upheaval and tumultuous change. You can be assured that in the presence of Jesus, at the footstool of His grace, you will find mercy, strength for change and the abundance of power you need to move forward.

The rewards of a repentant heart are joy and peace in the midst of upheaval and tumult. God has designed an abundant life for you. It is filled with the blessings of living in His constant presence, surrounded and protected by His love. His grace provides all that is needed in this time of change. His power is available to all who are positioned before the Throne of Grace in humility and adoration. Even if the known world should crumble apart, those who bow at the footstool of Jesus and accept His grace will remain whole before Him, hidden in His love.

> *Let us then fearlessly and confidently and boldly draw near to the throne of grace (the throne of God's unmerited favor to us sinners), that we may receive mercy [for our failures] and find grace to help in good time for every need [appropriate help and well-timed help, coming just when we need it]. Hebrews 4:16 (Amplified Bible)*

Instruments of Righteous Judgment

The Lord has called all those who believe in Him to be scepters of His righteousness in the earth. You are a scepter in His hand to extend love and mercy as you intercede for God's justice upon evil. David understood this principle quite well. He was a valiant warrior and wise king who knew that evil left unchallenged would consume his beloved Israel. He had no trouble praying for the intervention of the Lord in matters of state. He often called upon the Lord to bring destruction upon evil rulers or betraying comrades. He prayed and God moved with His wisdom.

In the life of Jesus, we see these same contrasts of compassion and righteous wrath. He spoke of turning the other cheek, but He also violently disrupted the greedy moneychangers in the temple. He was adamantly merciful toward men and women, but also adamantly opposed to the corruption and destruction caused by evil. Jesus exhorted His disciples to be "wise as serpents, and harmless as doves." (Matthew 10:16)

As a disciple of Christ, you must learn to judge, according to the discernment of the Holy Spirit, when you are to call forth God's mercy and when you are to call forth His justice.

The effective, fervent prayer of a righteous man avails much. Elijah was a man with a nature like ours, and he prayed earnestly that it would not rain; and it did not rain on the land for three years and six months. And he prayed again, and the heaven gave rain, and the earth produced its fruit. James 5:16-18

166

Elijah perceived, by the power of the Holy Spirit, that the judgment of God was necessary to bring the nation back to a righteous place before God. The Lord will reign over evil through the righteous prayers of the saints. Just as you intercede for the salvation of individuals, you must pray for the salvation of nations. Evil leaders cannot continue to work against the plans of the Creator and hinder a whole nation from receiving the blessings of God.

When the populace of a nation is being dulled by the ignorance and rebellion of a few, God will intervene with judgment to wake them up to the reality that He alone is God and He alone is Savior. You are called, as a disciple of Christ, to listen with a pure heart for the wise judgments of the Lord. They are mercy for nations and salvation for individuals. Your prayers can turn the tide of a nation away from evil and toward righteousness.

As you bow at the footstool of the Lord, He will raise you up with an innocent heart to reign with Him through righteous, fervent prayer that brings forth mercy and justice. It is time for the army of the Lord to rise up individually and corporately before the Throne of God and receive the wisdom and authority to turn nations away from evil toward the Living King of Glory.

Higher Wisdom

In Paul's first letter to the Corinthian church, he admitted his fearfulness in coming to them with the message of Christ. He did not present his message in eloquent words, but spoke simply and straightforwardly. But those words were accompanied with demonstrations of power so that their faith would not rest upon Paul's wisdom, but in the power of God. He also stated that he brought a different message of higher wisdom to the *spiritually mature Christians.*

Yet when we are among the full-grown (spiritually mature Christians) who are ripe in understanding, we do impart a [higher] wisdom (the knowledge of the divine plan previously hidden); but it is indeed not a wisdom of this present age...But rather what we are setting forth is a wisdom of God once hidden [from the human understanding] and now revealed to us by God—[that wisdom] which God devised and decreed before the ages for our glorification [to lift us into the glory of His presence].... Yet to us God has unveiled and revealed them by and through His Spirit, for the [Holy] Spirit searches diligently, exploring and examining everything, even sounding the profound and bottomless things of God [the divine counsels and things hidden and beyond man's scrutiny].... But we have the mind of Christ (the Messiah) and do hold the thoughts (feelings and purposes) of His heart. 1 Corinthians 2:6-16 (Amplified Bible)

In this hour, the Lord is calling His Church into the higher places of wisdom in His presence. You must seek His higher ways in intimate relationship so you can walk on the earth as a genuine reflection of His glory. To really exhibit the "mind of Christ" that you indeed have as God's child, you must be intimately related to the whole Trinity—Father, Son and Holy Spirit. These higher realms of truth and power come only through fellowship by and through the Holy Spirit having free access to every part of your life.

The Church is being summoned to a higher place of relationship and responsibility so that we can enjoy and express freely all the character of our Father. The world is looking for the One True God of creation and He has called us to prepare the way for Him to be seen and experienced in the world.

THE SECRET PLACE

My presence fills up the secret place.

My glory spills out in abundant grace.

Wisdom is found in My secret place.

Anointing discovered before My face.

Wars are fought first in the secret place,

Then, victory comes in the open space.

True love is fulfilled in My secret place

Then poured out through hearts filled with My grace.

Questions for reflection:

How do these scriptures affect your current view of God?

What feelings arise when you think about living a life like Jesus did on earth?

How have you experienced God's grace to make difficult choices between good and evil?

PSALM 110:7

He will drink of the brook by the way;
therefore will He lift up His head [triumphantly].

CHAPTER NINE

TRIUMPHANT KING

In the preceding verses of Psalm 110, David recorded the declarations of Father God over His Son, Jesus Christ. He declared His intention to make all the adversaries of Jesus become a footstool for His presence. He declared the description of a willing people who volunteer to live as scepters of righteousness and cover the earth in the day of His power. He declared Jesus to be the High Priest in a kingdom of kings and priests. And He declared the righteous acts of Jesus, the Judge, upon kings and nations who do not bow before Him in honor of His sovereign majesty.

Finally, in the last verse of this prophetic psalm, David recorded the strategy the Lord Jesus will use to usher His triumphant governmental authority into the earth. The plan is not complicated. It is simple, profound and amazing. Those who were once His enemies will become the power reserve for the completion of God's awesome plan of perfection.

His Sovereign Strategy

In John 14:6, Jesus declared, **"I am the Way, the Truth and the Life."** Those who follow Jesus, as disciples, are considered to be living in "the Way." In John 7:37-39, Jesus reveals an amazing fact about the people who believe in Him.

> *"If anyone thirsts, let him come to Me and drink. He who believes in Me, as the Scripture has said, out of his heart will flow rivers of living water." But this He spoke concerning the Spirit, whom those believing in Him would receive; for the Holy Spirit was not yet given, because Jesus was not yet glorified.*

Jesus prophesied, before His death and resurrection, about the gift of the Holy Spirit given to those who would believe on Him and follow Him. Through their faith in Jesus as their Savior King they would be filled with the Holy Spirit and overflow with **living water.** This same living water becomes "the brook by the wayside" refreshing and exalting Jesus as the King of glory.

David prophetically declared the nature and power available to a people who have become a footstool for the presence of Jesus. As they abide in His presence, His own power is poured through them, increasing His strength and might in the earth. This people, both individually and corporately, become the Body of Christ on earth.

This Body of Christ is not just a representation of Jesus. It is the divinely connected and positioned working flesh of the King of Glory. This Body knows no separation from the Head. There is no distance between the One who rules from

174

the Throne of Heaven and the ones who rule in the earth. The connection between Christ and His Body is powerful and eternal.

When Jesus was crucified, He left a group of twelve weak men behind to continue the work He had begun. Through the power of the Holy Spirit, these men were able to turn the world upside down, performing miracles, confronting religious and governmental authorities with the same confidence and power that Jesus exhibited.

The Holy Spirit became the divine connector between heaven and earth. His presence provided the power for the Body of Christ to remain vitally attached to the Vine of Life. There is no distance in the Spirit. Jesus is present in the earth through the Spirit-filled people who continue in "the Way."

Those who are thirsty for God are satisfied by drinking in the presence of Jesus, and Jesus is satisfied by drinking in the presence of those in "the Way." He is lifted up as the Head by those who bow at His feet.

This amazing principle is reflected in the natural cycle of water in the earth's atmosphere. The clouds release their moisture upon the earth and the plants and animals of the earth are filled and nourished by the water. The water on the earth itself evaporates into the atmosphere forming more clouds that eventually release their moisture once again onto the earth.

When the living water of God's word is received by thirsty hearts, His love and ministry nourishes and revives failing spirits. These refreshed souls lift their heads in praise and worship. Their praise and worship is released at His feet and He lifts His head in response to their adoration. Then He

175

releases new power and might into them causing His life to be increased within their hearts.

As this receiving and releasing relationship continues, these disciples of Christ are able to release His words of life to those they influence. As they receive them, the cycle of Living Water begins again. The power of His life is multiplied throughout the earth causing Him to triumph victoriously! What an amazing process!

Perpetuating the Cycle

This cycle of Living Water is glorious to ponder. But I'm sure you, like me, experience times of drought and famine in your life that seem to cut off the flow. Circumstances and temptations creep into your life and many times hinder your intimacy with the Lord. If you are distracted by them, you will tend to believe the Lord has somehow moved and is no longer pouring out His presence upon you.

You can mistakenly believe that if you are not perpetually producing or performing outward acts of service for God, you are no longer in good standing with the Lord. You can also begin to use your own actions as a measuring tape of your relationship with God.

The flow of intimacy is not measured by your circumstances or your service. It is measured by the fruit your life produces. The fruit is the character of Jesus formed in your spirit and displayed through your lifestyle. Fruit is a natural product of a thriving tree. True intimacy with the Father, Son and Holy Spirit will naturally produce the character of Jesus in your life.

Holy intimacy will not produce unholy fruit. It will display itself in every facet of your life. Intimacy with God is an eternal relationship beginning with a seed of faith and growing into a strong and fruitful tree, providing life and health to those who partake of it.

Even in your weakest moments, intimacy with the Lord can be experienced at the deepest levels. David wrote many of his psalms in places of defeat, discouragement and sorrow. God uses your fiery trials to forge His strength and excellence into your life.

177

In *My Utmost for His Highest*, Oswald Chambers addresses this struggle often encountered in intimate relationships with the Lord:

> *Do not rejoice in this, that the spirits are subject to you, but rather rejoice because your names are written in heaven. Luke 10:20*
>
> *Jesus Christ is saying here, "Don't rejoice in your successful service for Me, but rejoice because of your right relationship with Me." The trap you may fall into in Christian work is to rejoice in successful service—rejoicing in the fact that God has used you. Yet you will never be able to measure fully what God will do through you if you do not have a right-standing relationship with Jesus Christ. If you keep your relationship right with Him, then regardless of your circumstances or whoever you encounter each day, He will continue to pour "rivers of living water" through you (John 7:38). And it is actually by His mercy that He does not let you know it. Once you have the right relationship with God through salvation and sanctification, remember that whatever your circumstances may be, you have been placed in them by God. And God uses the reaction of your life to your circumstances to fulfill His purpose, as long as you continue to "walk in the light as He is in the light" (1 John 1:7).*
>
> *Our tendency today is to put the emphasis on service. Beware of the people who make their request for help on the basis of someone's usefulness. If you make usefulness the test, then Jesus Christ was the greatest failure who ever lived. For the saint, direction and guidance come from God Himself, not some measure of that saint's usefulness. It is the work that God does through us that counts, not what we do for Him. All that our Lord gives His attention to in a person's life is that*

person's relationship with God—something of great value to His Father. Jesus is "bringing many sons to glory..." (Hebrews 2:10).[1]

If you continue to bow at His footstool and surrender to His authority in these times of trial and testing, the Lord will produce His holy character in your spirit. That holiness cannot help but produce good fruit.

Intimacy is intentional not mechanical. Intimacy is natural not contrived. Intimacy is normal for those who trust the Lord and believe in His name. True intimacy will perpetuate the cycle of Living Water.

True Worship Models

David was a true worshiper. He began His worship in the sheepfold, but one of his greatest acts of worship was seen as he hid in the cave of Adullam. Strangely, it was not an act of battle skill or musical ability the Lord deemed as true worship. It was a wasted blessing that became a pinnacle of worship unto His God.

> *And the troop of Philistines encamped in the Valley of Rephaim. David was then in the stronghold, and the garrison of the Philistines was then in Bethlehem. And David said with longing, "Oh, that someone would give me a drink of the water from the well of Bethlehem, which is by the gate!" So the three mighty men broke through the camp of the Philistines, drew water from the well of Bethlehem that was by the gate, and took it and brought it to David. Nevertheless he would not drink it, but poured it out to the Lord. And he said, "Far be it from me, O Lord, that I should do this! Is this not the blood of the men who went in jeopardy of their lives?" Therefore he would not drink it. 2 Samuel 23:13-17*

At first glance, you might look at David's response as a ridiculous act of wastefulness. You might even say it was a slap in the face of those who risked their lives to bring him his heart's desire. But to God it was a beautiful expression of true thankfulness and humility for David to pour out the precious water to His Lord.

Even the men who had lovingly brought him the water, at their own great expense, may have reeled in disappointment. Their beloved leader would not partake of their selfless offering. But I am confident they eventually understood the honor and the humility David exhibited in pouring out the drink before the Lord. It cost them all dearly, but God was pleased and refreshed by this sincere act of worship set before Him.

Another infamous act of true worship is recorded in the Gospels:

> *And when Jesus was in Bethany at the house of Simon the leper, A woman came to Him having an alabaster flask of very costly fragrant oil, and she poured it on His head as He sat at the table. But when His disciples saw it, they were indignant, saying, "Why this waste? For this fragrant oil might have been sold for much and given to the poor." But when Jesus was aware of it, He said to them, "Why do you trouble the woman? For she has done a good work for Me. For you have the poor with you always, but Me you do not have always. For in pouring this fragrant oil on My body, she did it for My burial. Assuredly, I say to you, wherever this gospel is preached in the whole world, what this woman has done will also be told as a memorial to her. Matthew 26:6-14*

Jesus received this woman's selfless act of worship and even prophesied her act would be a memorial to her in the generations to come. She suffered severe criticism from the disciples for her costly expression, but Jesus praised her extravagant worship. He was blessed and prepared for the agony of His death on the cross through her abundant outpouring of love and adoration. Her worship lifted His head for the journey ahead.

On the day of Pentecost, after the death and resurrection of Christ, the apostles and others were gathered in Jerusalem to pray as Jesus had instructed them. The following outpouring of power by the Holy Spirit came as a result of their obedience and worship of Christ.

> *And they were all filled (diffused throughout their souls) with the Holy Spirit and began to speak in other (different, foreign) languages (tongues), as the Spirit kept giving them clear and loud expression [in each tongue in appropriate words]....*
>
> *And when this sound was heard, the multitude came together and they were astonished and bewildered, because each one heard them [the apostles] speaking in his own [particular] dialect. Acts 2:4-6 (Amplified Bible)*

This filling of the Holy Spirit and outpouring of tongues captured the attention of an entire city of people visiting from many different places. This was only the beginning of a true worship expression that ignited the early church and sent them to the ends of the earth with the message of Christ Jesus, the King of Kings and Savior of the world.

The Holy Spirit breathed new life and commitment into a group of disciples who were bowed in sincere worship of Christ, their Messiah and Risen Lord. He is still breathing spirit and truth into all who bow at the footstool of the King in adoration and reverence. Holy Spirit is empowering true worshipers every day to do the exploits of Jesus and even greater. And the Head (Christ) is lifted triumphantly as He drinks from the brook of living water that flows out from His Body (the church).

182

Deeper Waters

*As the hart pants and longs for the water brooks,
so I pant and long for you, O God. My inner self thirsts
for God, for the living God. When shall I come and behold the face of God?....[Roaring] deep calls to
[roaring] deep at the thunder of Your water-spouts; all
Your breakers and Your rolling waves have gone over
me. Psalm 42:1, 2, 7*

In this Psalm, you can hear the longing in the psalm-
ist's spirit to experience the intimate and life-giving presence
of his God. He is in a place of desperation for more of God
than he has known before. He cries from the depth of his being for a deeper place in God's heart. He cries out for the deep
living water from God's heart to carry him through the circumstances attempting to overwhelm him and undermine his
faith.

I believe this cry is a prophetic expression of all who
find themselves lacking the strength and power of God to face
trials and tribulations they encounter in life on earth. The
challenge to exhibit and express the life of Christ is only going to get harder in the days ahead. Darkness is increasing, but
the Light of Christ in His followers is going to get brighter as
we go deeper in relationship with the Father.

Recently, in a corporate prayer meeting, the Holy
Spirit began to expand the revelation of Jesus drinking from
the rivers of living water flowing out of the spirits of the Body
of Christ. We were fervently praying for the deep waters of
revelation to come into our hearts. I saw the river of God
flowing out from under the Throne of God. Many have been

183

sitting at His feet being washed with that river of revelation. Now I believe He is calling us to dive into the river and swim up into the ocean that resides under the Throne, the seat of His authority. The ocean is hidden deep in the heart of the Father.

To abide in His heart means to live underneath His authority (Throne) in a hidden reservoir of revelation and power. We cannot breathe the air of earth in this place. Our oxygen will come out of the living water that fills this reservoir of God. We will become like fish immersed in this ocean of living water. We will not survive on the oxygen of the temporal, but we will be sustained in the air of His eternal presence.

This picture is indeed strange, but all things are possible with the Lord. He desires you to drink deeply from the river of living water that flows from the Father's heart. And He desires you to abide continually in the ocean of His love and authority that feeds that river. Therefore, He will raise His head triumphantly in the days ahead.

True Greatness

There is a desire in each of us to do something great. God has deposited in us a capacity for greatness. We are drawn to those who do things out of the ordinary realm of living. The Lord challenged my thinking about greatness in the wee hours of the morning with one simple statement. I was veiled in a cloud of deep sleep, when suddenly awakened by these words, "To love is greatness."

Instantly the veil of sleep was lifted and my mind became alert. What did that mean? Where did that thought come from? As I pondered the words, I realized the Lord had spoken to my heart. I knew He was addressing an issue I needed to consider.

Greatness seems to be one of those illusive concepts with multiple definitions. Some may see a unique artist as great. Others think holding public office requires greatness. Sports enthusiasts esteem their favorite champions with greatness. Music lovers bestow greatness on their favorite performers or composers. Webster's dictionary defines greatness as large in number, size, skill or nobility.

As I have considered this idea of greatness, many men and women of the past have come to mind. Their lives expressed qualities that influenced and guided many into experiencing a better way of life.

Mother Theresa was surely a great woman. However, her lifestyle was one of simplicity and sacrifice. She worked tirelessly for the poorest of the poor, the extremely ill and the downtrodden of humanity. She traveled the world and expressed her love for God through her merciful acts of servitude. She fearlessly interceded on behalf of those she sought to help with prayer and through speaking on their behalf to all who would listen.

Abraham Lincoln was a man most would consider great, especially in the United States. His wisdom and influence as president during this country's most disruptive period of history continues to speak to us today. Even though he led us into a bloody and destructive war, an entire nation was set free from the horrors of slavery. His leadership opened the way for our nation to truly become a world leader.

However, Lincoln's life before the presidency was one full of political failure and personal emotional upheaval. He had no formal education and his appearance often made him the brunt of many jokes. He never won a political race until he became president and he suffered many financial failures. But all these personal trials seemed to strengthen his character and enable him to lead an adolescent country into a new era of reform. His love for law and justice empowered him to overcome seemingly insurmountable odds and reach a place of great influence.

The criteria for greatness varies in the minds of men. But God has only one simple explanation of greatness—love. His highest expression of love is embodied in the life of His Son, Jesus Christ. Yet Jesus did not display skills or talents men deem as great. He never wrote a book, composed a song or won any sort of competition. He did not hold a public office, start a business or have any worldly authority to influence others. Most of His life was lived in quiet obscurity. Very little is known about His childhood that would have signaled He was destined for greatness.

186

Jesus's entry into the earth was only celebrated by a small group of uneducated shepherds, three astrologers, His mother and father and a few barn animals. The angels, of course, joyfully heralded His birth to the shepherds, but no one else on earth witnessed their extravagant display of celebration. By the world's standards, He was an illegitimate child born to a common woman.

Jesus lived the last three years of His short life in the midst of turmoil, criticism and controversy. The religious leaders of that day believed He was a heretic. The government saw Him as a traitor. Some of His own family members thought He was crazy.

But in the midst of this cloud of hatred that followed Jesus everywhere he went, twelve men were overwhelmed by His words and trusted His instructions. As they followed Him from town to town, they intimately observed and experienced His greatness—His love. They watched as He drew others to Himself by healing the sick, delivering the demon-possessed and changing the character of notorious sinners.

Not only did these men witness His extreme acts of mercy to the needy, they observed His jealous zeal for the sanctity of the house of God. He violently overturned the tables of the moneychangers and drove them out of the temple. His love for Father God and His plans was expressed through Jesus's anger toward those who would defile the house of God.

Jesus also expressed His love for true righteousness by confronting the religious hypocrites of His day. The Pharisees time and time again accused Jesus of using the wiles of the devil to perform miracles. His love for the work of the

Holy Spirit rose up as He called them what they truly were, "You offspring of vipers!" (Matthew 12:34)

He did not defend His own actions, but stood up for righteousness and holiness as He expressed it through the power of the Holy Spirit. His love for true righteousness found a voice that stung the hearts of evil men and exposed their deceptive practices. Harsh words became an expression of His great love in the face of religious hypocrisy.

True love has a passionately fiery bent. When love is challenged and threatened, the expression takes on a heat that burns those who stand in its way. Those who express deep love are often labeled "fanatical" or "extremist." Passionate lovers are often misunderstood and thought to be foolish. Deep love can cause the lover a great deal of pain, but the pain cannot wipe out the devotion they carry.

More than ever, we need models of greatness. Extravagant expressions of love for God and man in true holiness could deeply impact the future of our nations. The next generation is at great risk of facing devastating consequences as a result of the poor examples of leadership and authority present today. But greatness expressed through loving, merciful and courageous acts of discipline, accountability and bold leadership could halt the obvious disruption of peace and wisdom we are experiencing. Greatness could restore our homes and countries to places of honor in the eyes of our Creator and the world.

"To love is greatness." The Lord is calling His people to a deeper place of devotion to His Son. Greatness surrounds Him and we cannot escape it if we live in His presence. I am convinced that God is calling all who believe on His name through faith in Christ Jesus to this place of greatness—the sincere love of God.

Psalm 110 will be played out to the fullest because the Lord Himself has declared it. The Father will fulfill His promise to the Son and the Body of Christ will be fully united with Christ as He makes all His enemies a footstool for His feet.

Will you take the plunge into the ocean of revelation and power deep within His heart? Will your generation be one in which He can drink deeply and be satisfied? Will He raise His head triumphantly on your watch?

PRAYER

Father God, in the mighty and powerful name of Jesus, I cry out to You to grace me to dive into Your heart with fearless abandon. I pray that You will be satisfied with the living water that flows out of me into the earth and into Your presence. Make me Your footstool and rest Yourself in my heart. May Jesus raise up His head triumphantly in my lifetime on earth. Amen.

Questions for reflection:

What motivates you to serve God?

Gratefulness for what He has done for me!

What is your personal definition of greatness?

How have you experienced the filling of the Holy Spirit?

CONCLUSION

Heaven is My throne, and the earth is My footstool.
What kind of house would you build for Me?
And what kind can be My resting place?
Isaiah 66:1

CHAPTER TEN

THE RESTING PLACE OF GOD

I believe God Himself answered these questions to Isaiah even before He asked them. He answered them through the record of a shepherd boy who took the time and made the effort to listen with his spiritual ears and see with his spiritual eyes what our loving God wants to reveal to those who would follow Him.

Psalm 110 is the song of redemption God shared with David to be passed down from generation to generation. This song declares God's desire to partner with imperfect men and women to restore fallen creation to His original glorious design. He opened the windows of heaven so an imperfect man could see into the future and witness His amazing plan of redemption for mankind. David witnessed the consummation of God's genius plan in Jesus Christ as He was reunited with the Father on the Throne of Heaven.

It is truly amazing that the God of all creation would entrust this vision to a sinful man to be shared with the world. It is just another display of the amazing grace of God towards His created ones. He delights to fellowship and work with His creation to display His glory and goodness. He reaches out to fallen man day after day to draw them back into intimate relationship with Himself.

Psalm 110 also declares the Lord's intent to commission a voluntary host of men and women to carry the scepter of His power and authority throughout all the earth. These intimate followers will display His goodness and greatness through prayer and action. They will reflect His mercy and His might as they influence others to come out of darkness into the marvelous light of His glory and grace. They will do the very things Jesus did and even greater as they move in obedience to cover the face of the earth. They will carry the very presence of God Himself to a lost and dying world.

Finally, Psalm 110 reveals the astounding plan of God to turn His enemies into the Body of Christ that will be joined to Jesus, the Head. This body of believers will be the very drink of refreshing that lifts the Head of the King of kings as He triumphantly possesses creation once again. As the Father promised, He will make the enemies of Jesus the very footstool of His presence in the earth. The very ones who betrayed Him in the garden are being restored so they can follow their God once again. Redeemed mankind will become the resting place of God!

The footprint of God is everywhere in the earth. Creation shouts His presence from the heights of heaven to the depths of the hidden recesses of earth. God has come to make His presence known to man whom He fashioned in His very own image.

Mankind carries the imprint of God's presence. You were designed to look and behave like the Creator. But more intimately, you were designed to become the permanent dwelling place of His character and power. No other creature carries that privilege and responsibility. The heart of man was specifically molded to be home to the One True God and all that He is.

His desire is for you to become more than just a tent to house and display His likeness. He desires sons and daughters who delight to imitate and display His glory. He desires for you to eagerly enjoy His presence in continual fellowship and intimacy. He longs to share His secret desires and strategies of power with you just as He has with Jesus and the Holy Spirit.

The united, inseparable trio of Father, Son and Holy Spirit created man as the overflow of their union and communion with each other. Their perfect oneness could not be contained within themselves. They chose to create men and women as vessels to fill with their continually expanding perfection. From the resting place of your heart, God can rule and reign with joy everywhere you place your feet. His power and authority begins to take ground as you follow in His footsteps of righteousness and glory.

God in all His majesty is not satisfied to live alone in His glorious throne room in heaven. He desires to have a family who shares all the riches of His glory! Who can resist such a relationship? Will you bow in reverence and gratitude to your Creator who longs to be your Father, Brother, Comforter, Friend, Nurturer and Bridegroom? Can you remain an enemy of God and resist becoming the resting place of His presence?

Fresh and Familiar

As I end this book, I am realizing that the truths I have shared may be quite new for some of you, while very familiar to others. I have been studying and learning most of these things for the last twenty-five years of my life. And as I have tried to convey the revelations I have gleaned, I am realizing I have only scratched the surface of a huge mountain of treasure the Lord wants to give all who call on His name.

The following words Jesus spoke are taking on a whole new meaning for me as I continue to explore my relationship with Him:

> ...Therefore every teacher and interpreter of the Sacred Writings who has been instructed about and trained for the kingdom of heaven and has become a disciple is like a householder who brings forth out of his storehouse treasure that is new and [treasure that is] old [the fresh as well as the familiar]. Matthew 13:52 (The Amplified Bible)

In writing this book, the Lord has used my foundation in His written word to help me discover ways to communicate some fresh and familiar things about His amazing plan for His creation. He is training believers to live in fellowship with Him in the kingdom of heaven now. Every day, if you are attentive and listening, He graciously desires to give you fresh wisdom and understanding to live on earth as Jesus did—in constant communion with the Father. He desires to build up and secure your foundations so He can construct a life through you that will draw others to His presence.

There is always more to learn and experience in the presence of our Father, Savior and Holy Spirit. I realize this interpretation of Psalm 110 is limited by my own understanding at the present time. So I encourage and challenge you who have read it to search for yourselves and question Him often concerning the truth of His kingdom and the part you play in it. Your part is bigger than you can even imagine!

So dream big! Reach high! Dig deep and go for the gold!! You were created for greatness and goodness. You will only find it at the footstool of Jesus.

PRAYER FOR THE READER

Praying for you from Ephesians 3:19-21
(Amplified Bible):

May you experience the love of Christ
which passes knowledge;
that you may be filled with all the fullness of God.
Now to Him who is able to do exceedingly
abundantly above all
that we ask or think, according to the power
that works in us, to Him be glory in the church
by Christ Jesus to all generations, forever and ever.
Amen.

Questions for reflection:

How have your beliefs about God been challenged by the information in this book?

What are some things you believe you need to do differently in order to be more intimate with God?

How have you been encouraged by the revelations in Psalm110?

MORE FOOTSTOOL SCRIPTURES

Old Testament
1 Chronicles 28: 2
Psalm 99:5
Psalm 132:7
Isaiah 66:1
Lamentations 2:1

New Testament
Matthew 5:35; 22:44
Mark 12:36
Luke 20:43
Acts 2:35; 7:49
Hebrews 1:13; 10:13

Brian Simmons, author of The Passion Translation of the Bible, makes this statement about Psalm 110 in a footnote reference to the psalm: *This Psalm is applied to Christ in the New Testament where it is quoted more often than any other Old Testament passage.*

That makes me think it is a very important scripture to learn and understand. Christ, Himself, quoted from Psalm 110 which was noted in three of the four Gospels.

NOTES

Chapter 2

1. *Strong's Exhaustive Concordance of the Bible*, Hebrew and Chaldee Dictionary (McLean, Virginia: MacDonald Publishing Company) 11, #341.

2. *Webster's Seventh New Collegiate Dictionary* (Springfield, Massachusetts: G. & C. Merriam Company, 1965) 14.

3. *Strong's*, 107, #7272.

Chapter 3

1. W. E. Vine, M.A., *An Expository Dictionary of New Testament Words* (Old Tappan, New Jersey: Fleming H. Revell Company, 1966) 207.

2. *Strong's Exhaustive Concordance of the Bible*, Greek Dictionary of the New Testament (McLean, Virginia: MacDonald Publishing Company) 18, #922.

3. *Strong's*, 24, #1391.

Chapter 4

1. *Strong's Exhaustive Concordance of the Bible*, Hebrew and Chaldee Dictionary (McLean, Virginia: MacDonald Publishing Company) 38, #2398.

2. *Strong's*, 58, #3820.

3. *Strong's*, 55, #3629.

Chapter 5

1. *Strong's Exhaustive Concordance of the Bible*, Hebrew and Chaldee Dictionary (McLean, Virginia: MacDonald Publishing Company) 65, #4294.

Chapter 6

1. *Webster's Seventh New Collegiate Dictionary* (Springfield, Massachusetts: G. & C. Merriam Company, 1965) 845.

2. James Reimann, ed., My Utmost for His Highest, An Updated Edition In Today's Language (Discovery House Publishers) October 3.

3. Strong's Exhaustive Concordance of the Bible, Hebrew and Chaldee Dictionary (McLean, Virginia: MacDonald Publishing Company) 48, #3117.

4. Strong's, 39, #2428.

5. Strong's, 37, #2342.

Chapter 7

1. Strong's Exhaustive Concordance of the Bible, Hebrew and Chaldee Dictionary (McLean, Virginia: MacDonald Publishing Company) 112, #7650.

Chapter 9

1. James Reimann, ed., My Utmost for His Highest, An Updated Edition In Today's Language (Discovery House Publishers) August 30.

ABOUT THE AUTHOR

Angela Brown is a student and lover of the Word of God. She loves interceding in prayer and sharing her faith through writing and painting. She is the best-selling author of *Prayers that Avail Much for Children*, a prayer book based on Scripture created for young children. She has written articles for Christian periodicals and assisted other authors in compiling and writing their own publications. She has taught Bible studies for adults and children, spoken at women's retreats, led and participated in missions in Scotland, Hungary and Romania, and trained others for leadership in church settings. She has been an intercessor with the Word of Love ministry for over 25 years.

Angela is also the founder of Creative Catalysts, a small community of Christian artisans in her hometown. They meet monthly to study God's word, encourage each other in their creative giftings and learn how to better share their faith through their artistic endeavors in their local community and the world.

Angela and her husband, Jackie, have been married 47 years and reside in Marietta, Georgia. They have two daughters, two grandsons, one granddaughter-in-law and one great-grandson and a great-granddaughter on the way.